Further Praise for Teaching with Purpose

"There is no greater job than that of a teacher. *Teaching with Purpose: An Inquiry into the Who, Why, and How We Teach* inspires us to be the very best. Teachers have the opportunity to elevate their students to greatness; they have the opportunity to build relationships that support and nurture individual children, while also appreciating their diversity. James D. Kirylo offers a strong theoretical background while providing descriptions of best practices. This book is an inspiring resource that promises to offer teachers, and those studying teaching, the opportunity for self-reflection and the chance to refine their teaching." —**Jan Lacina**, PhD, Texas Christian University

"Kirylo has written a remarkable book in *Teaching with Purpose*. He inspires us to consider the well-being of every child and our privileged role as a teacher, which comes from a heart-centered approach. He lifts the teaching profession to a noble stature, one of love, faith, hope, humility, compassion, and persistence. He advocates for building relationships with students and believing that all students are unique and valued. He illuminates the influential power that teachers have. Teachers create purposeful opportunities by believing in the possibilities of each child. Thus, teaching is a human endeavor, and Kirylo masterfully humanizes the educational process." —**Sandra J. Stone**, EdD, professor emeritus, Northern Arizona University

"Kirylo skillfully reminds us of what constitutes as purposeful teaching at a time when test-taking seems to be valued over teaching students to become life-long learners. He pithily articulates the major principles that all teachers must bear in mind—that the rectitude of teaching depends on the teacher's disposition and ability to reflect, to build relationships with students, and to hone every child's natural talent and gifts so they may attain their full potential, all with a sound understanding that teaching is after all a political endeavor. Bravo!" —**Vidya Thirumurthy**, associate professor of education, Pacific Lutheran University

"In this time of teacher-bashing, Kirylo's book offers new hope. *Teaching with Purpose* describes teaching as the development of basic human virtues, including self-understanding, caring relationships, the ability to inspire, and attention to those most in need. This book will enhance both new and veteran teachers' appreciation of why the profession is so vital, while bringing them up-to-date on a wide variety of educational topics. This is a deeply satisfying book." —**William Crain**, professor of psychology, The City College of New York; author of *Theories of Development: Concepts and Applications*

"In *Teaching with Purpose*, career teachers are respected, celebrated, championed, and understood, and assessment is taken off of its undeserved pedestal and placed back into the skilled educator's toolbox where it belongs. This book is a refreshingly balanced read." —**Mercedes K. Schneider**, PhD, career teacher; author of *Common Core Dilemma—Who Owns Our Schools?*

"*Teaching with Purpose* inspired me in the same way I have been inspired by the writings of Nel Noddings, Elliot Eisner, and Parker Palmer. With a focus on who we are as teachers, why we teach, and how we teach, this exemplary book is a "must read" for all prospective, novice, and veteran teachers." —**Jerry Aldridge**, professor emeritus of education, University of Alabama at Birmingham

"In *Teaching with Purpose*, scholar and educator James D. Kirylo examines, in plain language, the deep ethics of teaching. Highly readable and eminently thoughtful, Kirylo's text emphasizes six key dispositions needed for the development of creative, humane teachers: love, faith, hope, humility, compassion, and persistence. Kirylo calls upon educators to live out such values in their teaching practice in order to evoke the humanity and intelligence in each student. Drawing on Freire's notion of teachers and students as "unfinished beings" whose ongoing formation is the project of critical pedagogy, as well as on Dewey's insistence that education is growth in life itself and not preparation for later living, Kirylo offers a text that will elevate all educators who pursue these transformational goals with him." —**Ira Shor**, professor of composition/rhetoric and urban education, City University of New York Graduate Center; author of *Empowering Education*; co-author with Paulo Freire of *A Pedagogy for Liberation*

"For too long, schools have been places young people go to watch their teachers work. Kirylo posits an alternative educational universe built on loving children, faith, hope, humility, compassion, and persistence. His message of equity, diversity, and social justice is a call to action for all of us who believe that empowerment of teachers and the opportunity of schooling is the driving force for the benefit of the common good. His blueprint should be on the reading list for new teachers, teacher educators, and policymakers who are busy inventing tests and standards on the deck of the *Titanic*." —**John Fischetti**, dean of education and head of school, University of Newcastle, Australia

"In *Teaching with Purpose*, Kirylo probes the complexity of what it means to teach and learn in today's schools. He shows that effective teaching is not just a matter of what teachers do, but also a matter of who they are and how they come to know their students. Drawing upon philosophy, history, and psychology, Kirylo reminds readers that, at its heart, high-quality education requires teachers to look deeply at their own identities while also grounding their pedagogy within the context of authentic relationships. This scholarly yet accessible text will both inform and inspire educators, as well as those who aspire to the profession." —**Patricia A. Crawford**, associate professor of early childhood education and language, literacy and culture, University of Pittsburgh

Teaching with Purpose

An Inquiry into the Who, Why, and How We Teach

James D. Kirylo

ROWMAN & LITTLEFIELD
Lanham • Boulder • New York • London

Published by Rowman & Littlefield
A wholly owned subsidiary of The Rowman & Littlefield Publishing Group, Inc.
4501 Forbes Boulevard, Suite 200, Lanham, Maryland 20706
www.rowman.com

Unit A, Whitacre Mews, 26-34 Stannary Street, London SE11 4AB

Copyright © 2016 by James D. Kirylo

All rights reserved. No part of this book may be reproduced in any form or by any electronic or mechanical means, including information storage and retrieval systems, without written permission from the publisher, except by a reviewer who may quote passages in a review.

British Library Cataloguing in Publication Information Available

Library of Congress Cataloging-in-Publication Data

Names: Kirylo, James D.
Title: Teaching with purpose : an inquiry into the who, why, and how we teach / James D. Kirylo.
Description: Lanham, Maryland : Rowman & Littlefield, 2016. | Includes bibliographical references.
Identifiers: LCCN 2016004761 (print) | LCCN 2016007397 (ebook) | ISBN 9781475812930 (cloth :
    alk. paper) | ISBN 9781475812947 (pbk. : alk. paper) | ISBN 9781475812954 (Electronic)
Subjects: LCSH: Teaching. | Education—Aims and objectives.
Classification: LCC LB1025.3 .R57 2016 (print) | LCC LB1025.3 (ebook) | DDC 371.102—dc23 LC
    record available at http://lccn.loc.gov/2016004761

∞ ™ The paper used in this publication meets the minimum requirements of American National Standard for Information Sciences Permanence of Paper for Printed Library Materials, ANSI/NISO Z39.48-1992.

Printed in the United States of America

*for all teachers whose chief focus is to inspire
students to fall in love with learning*

for all schools whose chief focus is learning, not scores

*for all school systems whose chief focus is
ensuring and expanding opportunity*

Contents

Preface	ix
Acknowledgments	xi
Introduction	xiii

Section I: From the Inside Out

1	An Earned Privilege	3
2	Establishing a Personal Philosophy of Education	7
3	The Decisive Relevance of Disposition: Reconciling the Private with the Public	13
4	Six Dispositions of Significance	17
5	Reflective Thinking— Thoughtful Action	25

Section II: Entering into Relationships

6	Hardwired to Be in Relationships: A Thing of the Brain	31
7	Fostering the Teacher–Student Relationship: From Right Where They Are	35
8	Cultivating Dialogue	39
9	The Flow of Integrity	43
10	Other Relationships: Parents/Caregivers, Colleagues, and the Wider Community	47
11	To Be in Relationships Is to Celebrate Diversity	53

Section III: The Goal Is to Inspire (An Artistic Endeavor)

12	The Character of Inspiration	61
13	Inspiration and the Autobiographical Nature of Teaching	67
14	Inspiration Leads to an Artistic Act	71

Section IV: The Glue That Is Educational Psychology

15	The Critical Relevance of Theory	77
16	Paving the Way Toward Child/Developmental Psychology: John Locke and Jean-Jacques Rousseau	81
17	An Overview of Behaviorism, Cognitivism, and Humanism	87

Section V: Five Components of Knowledge

18 Knowledge of Pedagogy and Knowledge of Classroom Management ... 97

19 Knowledge of Learning, Knowledge of Students, and Knowledge of Subject Matter ... 105

Section VI: Assessment Is to "Sit With"

20 Two Different Processes: Assessment and Evaluation ... 113
21 The Emergence of a Testing Movement ... 117
22 Moving into an Era of High-Stakes Testing ... 123
23 Four Harmful Effects of High-Stakes Testing ... 129
24 Emphasizing Formative and Portfolio Assessments ... 137

Section VII: Teacher as Leader: Hierarchy, Poverty, and the Village

25 Teacher as Leader ... 145
26 Teacher Leadership and the Greatest Challenge: Poverty ... 151
27 It Takes a Village ... 157

Appendix A ... 161
Appendix B ... 165
Appendix C ... 167
References ... 169
Index ... 181
About the Author ... 185

Preface

> *The process of contextualization invites us to understand and assess the complexity of the learning process in schools.*
>
> (Kincheloe, Slattery, and Steinberg 2000, 2)

If one ever wants to observe a glorious, yet a bit offbeat and even amusing sight, it is seeing a seven-year-old boy adorned with a football helmet, shoulder pads, oversized padded football pants, and cleats. The helmet appears to overwhelm the head, the uniform seemingly makes him abnormally larger in stature, and watching him run down the field with great determination with a large football in hand can be a mesmerizing moment.

Anthony did not know I attended this particular practice until the very end, during which the October red-orange sky was moving toward twilight. When he noticed I was standing and gazing through the fence, he excitingly bolted toward my direction as his large helmet bobbled up and down. When he got to the fence with his well-worn, white, grass-stained uniform, he peered through his helmet, shifting his eyes upward toward the eye opening of it, his nose and mouth obstructed from view by the face mask.

Looking up toward me, his little brown eyes tenderly greeted mine, prompting him to excitedly utter, "You came." "Of course," I responded back. And then Anthony ran off back to his teammates. He was happy; I was gratified, and he knew I came to that practice especially for him. This particular moment took place over twenty-five years ago.

Yet, as I think about it and relate this brief narrative here, I still burst with a great sense of retrospective affection, as I do when I reflect on the numerous other singular moments during my K–12 teaching experience. The spontaneous twinkle in Anthony's eyes and the warmth in my heart ignited a human connection. Truly, the sustenance that makes teaching meaningful is the humanity of it all.

Long before I read or heard about Parker Palmer and his perceptive book, *The Courage to Teach*, I have always reminded myself that I ultimately teach who I am. Palmer (2007) puts it this way: "We teach who we are" (1)—that is, the more I understand my motives, my moods, my weaknesses, my strengths, my biases, and the reflection and thinking that guide my action, the more likely I am able to make sense of the tangled complexity of teaching and learning, and the more likely I am able to make the connection between theory and practice.

To state another way, the more I understand my humanity, the more I am better able to make meaningful human connections with my diverse student population. Knowing thyself, to borrow from Socrates (though likely first uttered by Thales), implies an important agency to know and realize the other.

TEACHING AS A CONTEXTUALIZED AFFAIR

The autobiographical, social, cultural, relational, economical, and historical is indeed an uninterrupted, interconnected reality when one enters a classroom. The simple act of watching Anthony practice football connects my happiness for him to his own excitement that the sport brings him, linked to my concern about his struggling in school, which is associated with his apparent weary self-concept, which is then connected to the fact that his father is relatively absent, laboring to make ends meet, working two jobs, which is further coupled to the passing away of Anthony's mother. And that is only a part of Anthony's story, not to mention the individual stories of the other twenty-four students in the class, some of whom are more or less complicated than Anthony.

The above continuously unfolding portrait of life that reveals itself on a daily basis in a classroom is also contextually attuned to a larger picture of what it means to be a teacher. That is, to be contextually attuned to the larger picture is to possess essential understandings of the following critical aspects of teaching:

- The complexity of what it intimately means to be a teacher and its relationship with the other;
- The theoretical, pedagogical, and sociological underpinnings that inform the teaching and learning process;
- A fundamental awareness of the history, meaning, and purpose of assessment;
- The intent and action as to what it means to be a teacher-leader, particularly as it relates to the notion of critical pedagogy; and lastly,
- An awareness of one of the foremost challenges facing educators, which is the impact of poverty on young people, and to realize that a community effort is needed in order to address this challenge.

Driving the thematic trajectory of this text, the aforementioned critical aspects of teaching are distinct in and of themselves. Yet these themes are clearly interconnected, both collectively and contextually, informing the richness of what it means to teach with purpose.

—*James D. Kirylo*

Acknowledgments

Writing a book is a process that demands much energy, commitment, and focus, and the infusion of support and insight from others greatly graces and energizes that process. In that light, I would like to thank Jerry Aldridge for reading multiple drafts of this work; his insightful comments were extremely helpful. Thanks to Mary Banbury and Dixon Hearne for taking the time to carefully read early drafts and offer outstanding suggestions.

With respect to the themes related to neuroscience, John O'Reilly was particularly helpful in clarifying concepts. Also, thanks to Dayne Sherman, who was instrumental in inspiring me to underscore the notion of inspiration and its link to the teaching and learning process. With much gratitude to William Crain for his expertise, particularly in offering suggestions on the chapters related to child development, the work of Jean Piaget, John Locke, and others. A big thanks to Roseanna Atwell, who was especially helpful in preparing those countless articles for me to carefully read, and thanks to Pattie Steib for helping me sort through book cover possibilities. And it is with much appreciation to David Armand, writer extraordinaire, for his editorial assistance, and the great help he has been over the years.

Thank you Mercedes Schneider, John Fischetti, Ira Shor, Jan Lacina, Jerry Aldridge, William Crain, Vidya Thirumurthy, Patricia A. Crawford, and Sandra Stone for your most appreciated blurbs. I am humbled by this lineup of wonderful people who have so significantly contributed to the education profession.

I sincerely appreciate all the good folks at Rowman & Littlefield, especially Carlie Wall, Bethany Janka, and Will True. A big thanks to Tom Koerner, the vice president of education at Rowman & Littlefield. His patience and expertise in guiding me through the process of publication has been greatly appreciated.

And finally, and most importantly, the sun which shines my life, to my wife, Anette, and our two wonderful boys, Antonio and Alexander. I am forever grateful; forever the better; forever blessed.

Introduction

For five days a week for approximately nine months out of the year totaling countless hours, teachers work with other people's most treasured gifts—their children. That the teacher is the most important element in fostering an energetic, engaging, and inspiring classroom environment where authentic learning can unfold cannot be overstated.

Indeed, it is the teacher who understands self or does not; it is the teacher who is prepared or is not; it is the teacher who has command of subject matter or does not; it is the teacher who inculcates in an appropriate way or does not; and it is the teacher who is patient, understanding, empathetic, and enthusiastic—or is not.

What the above suggests is that there are multiple considerations inherent in the process that fosters purposeful teaching. That is, among other considerations, one must be aware of context in the careful examination of theories of human development, the nature of learning, the nature of knowledge, the notion of developmentally appropriate practice, the importance of dispositions, and the influence of the cultural, social, and economic forces that play into the pedagogical process (Parkay and Hass 2000).

To that end, there are five guiding assumptions that organizationally frame the chapter contents of this book. First, the idea of knowing one's self is the rudder that steers the direction of what it means to teach with purpose.

Coming to know self is not some navel-gazing endeavor, but rather a journey-in-process that naturally embraces the notion that we are unfinished beings who realize that in order to serve the other, it is critical to recognize the autobiographical nature inherent in teaching. An ongoing, honest, reflective understanding of our dispositions, attitudes, and perspectives is what determines the integrity of any tangible approach, method, or interaction. In short, foundational in nature, the first guiding assumption here is that we teach from the inside out.

Second, education is about entering into relationships. To state differently, education is about working with human beings and their dreams, goals, and aspirations. Teachers teach children, not a discipline or a subject matter, which is not a question of semantics.

Third, education is about opportunity, implying that our schooling focus must be one that works to maximize student possibilities through an approach that works to tap into the variety of gifts, talents, and potential of every student.

Fourth, the chief task of the teacher is to inspire. Because the notion of inspiration is what moves us to be and to do, inspirational teachers ignite students to intrinsically aspire toward accomplishment. Fifth, education is a political enterprise, and whether discussing matters related to curriculum, assessment, pedagogy, class size, or any number of educational issues, it is important for teachers to be well-informed and to be involved in the political process.

In the final analysis, teachers who teach from the inside out are those who engagingly approach their craft with demonstrative purpose, seeking to make meaningful connections with students. And this teaching act never occurs in a vacuum; but rather it is an endeavor that is always existentially contextualized.

Therefore, the fundamental purpose of this book is to underscore what it means to be a teacher, the critical aspects that intersect the teaching and learning process, and the multiple considerations that teachers must deliberate in order to teach with purpose.

The arrangement of this book is formatted in seven broad sections, with each section comprised of relevant chapters, each succinctly written. Short chapters can be aesthetically pleasing, and tend to be uncomplicatedly reader-friendly.

Moreover, the seven sections that comprise the book can thematically stand alone, meaning that sequentially reading this text is not necessarily required. But in its totality (however one chooses to proceed), the seven thematic sections are ultimately intertwined, which work to conceptually and contextually ground a teacher's thinking, relationships, and action.

WRITING APPROACH AND INTENDED AUDIENCE

The writing approach of *Teaching with Purpose* is naturally written in an academic tone, yet mindful of reader accessibility in order to be attractive to a wide-range audience. In addition, while the text does provide some practical ideas in respective chapters, the intent of this book is not so much to provide a methodology or "do" and "don't" tips, but rather to paint a picture of seven broad essential understandings that are critical in order to better conceptually and contextually teach with a sense of purpose.

As a for-your-information point, a question section at the end of each section has not been included as is seen in many books on education such as this. And while question sections may have their place in such books, these sections have generally struck me as contrived and artificial. That is, thoughtful people don't need a "question" section to spark exploration; rather, thoughtful people continuously question as they read books and read life itself.

To be sure, there is a certain relevance of this book for all K-12 educators, but the particular targeted audience is geared toward elementary school teachers who are continuously seeking to refine their craft. Moreover, teacher educators may incorporate the text for a variety of education courses.

For example, the text can be on the required reading list for education graduate courses, such as a curriculum, diversity, or pedagogy class. The work can also be used for an upper level undergraduate education course where prospective teachers will get a realistic and critical view as to what it means to be a teacher. School systems may be interested in using this text for professional development types of venues. Finally, this book may be a good resource for policy makers, parents/caregivers, and others who have a general interest in education.

Section I

From the Inside Out

Education, therefore, is a process of living and not a preparation for future living.

(Dewey 1964b, 430)

ONE
An Earned Privilege

It is safe to say there is nothing parents hold more precious than their children, and they must, by law, entrust them physically and emotionally to virtual strangers (also known as "schoolteachers") for most of their waking hours, for a sequence of months and years.

(Manvell 2009, 12–13)

The purpose of education is for people to learn. And during the approximate six- to seven-hour school day, a teacher instructs, guides, facilitates, leads, disciplines, encourages, challenges, praises, talks, listens, circulates, sits, observes, and makes countless decisions. In fact, a teacher makes anywhere between 800–1,500 decisions daily (Kauchak and Eggen 2005).

A school year is generally around 180 days. Consider, therefore, the following: a teacher minimally interacts with her/his student population 1,170 hours during an entire academic year and, on the low end, makes 936,000 annual decisions, and on the high end 1,755,000. The presumption of holding such enormous power to make hundreds of decisions every day—averaging annually somewhere around the 1.3 million-mark—assumes that the educator is informed, qualified, and certified.[1]

At the end of the school day, while teachers may utter the final goodbye to the last student strolling out of the classroom, their day is not complete. There is a certain amount of classroom straightening up that beckons, papers to be graded are calling, lessons to prepare are waiting, and perhaps even phone calls to parents are necessary.

In fact, for classroom teachers, their day is never really complete; there is simply a daily deliberate stopping point on a constant continuum of activity. As if that were not enough, the greater challenge for teachers is to properly monitor their continuous stream of consciousness that thinks about their students and the numerous decisions they have made and are going to make that impact those students' cognitive, psychological, emotional, and physical well-being.

Musings about students abound in the teacher's mind: the one who is brilliantly excelling; the one who arrives to school hungry; the one who comes to school unprepared; the one who demonstrates intermittent sparks of creative energy; the one who thrives on seeking attention through inappropriate behavior; the one who is unkempt; and the one who seems to be a loner.

While some students in a teacher's mind may stand out more than others for a variety of different reasons, the fact is that each student uniquely defines herself/himself in some distinct way. The task of the teacher, therefore, is to discern that uniqueness, which is a reflective process that unfolds as a result of thoughtful observation, interaction, and discernment—in and out of school.

What the above suggests is that being an educator is indeed a way of being. It is a way of being how teachers conduct themselves in actual classroom practice. It is a way of being how they prepare for that practice. It is a way of being how they justly assess and evaluate their students. It is a way of being how they organize time, priorities, and tasks. It is a way of being how they communicate and relate. It is a way of being how they think. It is a way of being how they go about the process of making decisions. It is a way of being how they view people as individuals, process their conceptions related to diversity, and capture the relativeness of what it means to recognize uniqueness.

It is for those aforementioned reasons why many view the idea of becoming a teacher as a vocation, a term that has its roots in the Latin *vocare*, meaning "to call" or to summon. In other words, as a result of responding to a deep prompting or calling, one views the idea of being a teacher as a way of life, a way of being in order to make a difference. In short, while a job or career is prompted to *make* a living, a call is a prompt to *respond* to a way of life.

In this sense, there is a certain spiritual aspect that triggers a response to that summons, reaching to the very core of a teacher's being in sustaining his/her work with young people (Marshall 2009). Put another way, and notwithstanding the influence of others, the call to teach "ultimately comes from the voice of the *teacher within*, the voice that invites me to honor the nature of my true self" (Palmer 2007, 30, author's emphasis).

In vulnerability, expectation, and hope, parents daily turn over their most precious gifts—their own children—into the hands of the teacher, which assumes s/he possesses credibility, qualification, expertise, and a deep desire to teach. To state differently, turning over one's child to a teacher's hands is an act of sacred trust, for the teacher is responsible for nurturing an educative environment that appropriately fosters the cognitive, physical, psychological, emotional, and even spiritual well-being of a child. In the end, therefore, being called "teacher" is an earned privilege. And a teacher initially earns that privilege by recognizing that "call" to become a teacher. But that is just the beginning.

With integrity, pride, and competency, that call is imbued with a sense of great responsibility and a realization of the critical importance of professional autonomy that fosters a culture of love, joy, and justice (Purpel 1989). Moreover, a part of that process of realizing the earned privilege of becoming a teacher is entering a quality teacher-education program that faithfully, skillfully, systematically, and meticulously honors the process of what it means to be called "teacher." Indeed, first-rate teacher-education programs are integral in fostering the professionalization of teaching and are key in better enabling high-quality teaching (Darling-Hammond 2006a, 2006b).

And, finally, once teacher candidates are declared qualified and certified to teach, they intimately come to learn this privileged journey requires one to live an examined life. Among other interrelated processes, this examined life realizes the significance and place of having a personal philosophy of education, the theme of the next chapter.

NOTE

1. Within the confines of a classroom, teaching can be a "solitary" event between teacher and students in which hundreds of daily decisions are made; however, this does not preclude the notion that a classroom community can be a place where a teacher fosters a democratic space in which students are included in decision making. Moreover, it is not uncommon that a classroom is a collaborative endeavor in which other professionals such as a speech, occupational, or a physical therapist or numerous other types of professionals share responsibility in making informed decisions with the teacher relative to student need.

TWO
Establishing a Personal Philosophy of Education

> *A philosophy of education is thus a most arduous undertaking. It is, however, an undertaking of vital importance, for upon it all intelligent decisions about educational matters ultimately rest.*
>
> (Cahn 1970, 1)

All schools generally have a mission statement, typically posted in prominent view for all to see. For example, a school may have a mission statement posted with large, blue, bolded letters that asserts something to the effect of, "the mission of ABC school is to prepare all students to participate in a global society."

Therefore, the question for the educators working in that school is to be clear about the values, beliefs, and approaches that ought to be taken in order to tangibly live that mission. And the question for students (and even their parents/caregivers) is to be witnesses of that mission in action and the kind of impact it is having.

For the mission of the school to bloom, there indeed needs to be a synergistic energy among educators, students, parents/caregivers, and the community at large. The assumption here is that the educators who work in a particular school must find value in furthering its mission.

While the fundamental idea of having an institutional mission statement is related to purpose (i.e., explaining why the school is here), a philosophy is more centered on what values, ways of being, and beliefs inform and drive that purpose. The point here is that while teachers naturally work in schools that proclaim a certain mission or purpose, each individual teacher, therefore, needs to carefully consider that mission, and how her/his personal philosophy of education resonates within that mission.[1] Moreover, when asked, can the teacher promptly respond to the question what her/his personal philosophy of education is? Furthermore, is that philosophy conspicuously posted in her/his classroom in a similar vein as a mission statement is displayed in a school?

It is probable that most reading this text have had to write their philosophy of education early on in one of their teacher-preparation courses, perhaps only to be filed away as a distant memory of a useful assignment once undertaken. And whether one remembers the substance of that assignment, or is deliberately aware of one's current philosophy, or continues to mentally refine his/her philosophy of education—consciously known or not—all educators possess a philosophy of education, ultimately demonstrated in action. To put another way, with intentional awareness or not, we teach what we value; we teach who we are.

For example, we can be sincere about our commitment to teaching, but we risk being sincerely wrong in our approach if we are lacking in philosophical awareness regarding why we are using a particular methodology and the kind of impact it is having on the teaching and learning process.

Conversely, if we are aware of the philosophy that guides our approach and we are grounded in practices that are developmentally appropriate, the likelihood of making meaningful connections with students is cultivated. It is only logical, therefore, to be intimately aware of our values, what we believe, and what drives the thinking that informs the pedagogical actions and interactions that are taken with students.

Enter in a personal philosophy of education. In making the case of the significant value of one's personal philosophy of life and its relationship to one's work as an educator, Webb, Metha, and Jordon (2007) explain:

> Whereas our personal philosophy of life enables us to recognize the meaning of our personal existence, our *philosophy of education* enables us to recognize certain educational principles that define our views about the learner, the teacher, and the school. To teach without a firm understanding of one's personal philosophy and philosophy of education would be analogous to painting a portrait without the rudimentary knowledge and skill of basic design, perspective, or human anatomy. (54, author's emphasis)

At its root, the word "philosophy" means a love and search of wisdom, and the root of education is related to "bringing out," to "lead."

In the search for wisdom to inform the self to better lead and bring out the best in the other, teachers must necessarily examine their epistemological, ontological, and axiological way of looking at the world. Infrequently blossoming in a vacuum, this process "requires rigorous thinking, extensive reading, ongoing dialogue, critical analysis, and intuitive reflection" (Kincheloe, Slattery, and Steinberg 2000, 27).

In order to move toward that end, concepts related to the nature of knowledge, nature of being, and nature of values will naturally be relevant and are linked to the notion of our unfinishedness in our quest to continually grow in awareness and informed action.

EPISTEMOLOGY

Epistemology examines the nature of knowledge, how we come to know, what is true, and what are the sources of knowledge. Epistemological inquiry thus considers a broad range of ways we come to know, such as through the divine, intuition, our senses, logic, experiences, directly, or indirectly. Indeed, the teacher who remains in that place of being epistemologically curious is able to connect the confluence of emotion, feeling, passion, cognition, intellectual rigor, and critical reasoning, realizing there are a variety of ways one comes to know (Freire 2007, 2005).

Guided by an epistemological curiosity provides for the teacher an integral tool to customize her/his pedagogical approach and to teach in such a way that is informed by what Kincheloe (2006) characterizes as a complex epistemology of practice. In this practice, the teacher "uses her wide set of understandings to examine the vicissitudes of the educational act. Such forms of practitioner cognition empower the teacher to change her practice by making reasoned interpretations of the situation she faces" (91).

ONTOLOGY

Ontology, which emerges from a branch of philosophy called metaphysics, examines our nature of being, why we are here, as well as our becoming. The ontological questions a teacher needs to consider are multiple: What is her/his purpose? What makes life meaningful? How does s/he view the other in relationship to herself/himself? Are human beings basically good or bad? What is her/his relationship to a supreme being or the supernatural? What are the forces that shape reality? What are the motives that impacted his/her decision to teach?

To be sure, these and other related ontological questions are ongoing and ones that require thoughtful consideration and reflection. And in the end, the principal ontological task of teachers is to foster the humanization (to be more fully human) of their students in order that they become subjects of their existence (as opposed to objects) in which they become participants in life (as opposed to spectators) (Freire 1998a, 1994a, 1990; Inglis 1959). As Roberts (2000) succinctly asserts, "the vocation of becoming more fully human is what defines us as human beings; it is the *essence* of being human" (45).

AXIOLOGY

Axiology is a strand of philosophy that considers the nature of values, subdivided into the area of ethics: what is "good" or "bad"; what is "right" or "wrong"; and aesthetics: what is of beauty and what is not? When it comes to making decisions of any kind; when confronted with challenges and dilemmas of any kind; and when it comes to determining appropriate/inappropriate behaviors, ways of speaking, and ways of doing, a teacher must be critically aware of the values, biases, and thinking that informs her/his actions and interactions with students.

EMBRACING OUR UNFINISHEDNESS

Epistemological, ontological, and axiological considerations and questions are not for the faint-hearted or the superficial. As teachers deliberate these various considerations, connecting them to their personal philosophies of education and then linking them to concrete action, they realize early on, as previously alluded to, the deep ongoing rigor involved in the process. And an energizing element in that process is to realize the integral place of what Freire (2007, 1998a) characterizes as our "unfinishedness."

That is, Freire saw life as an adventurous ontological search that was driven by his epistemological curiosity, and viewed through a certain axiological prism of the world. In other words, to draw from his viewpoint, with the assumption that one possesses an insatiable desire to learn, teachers who view themselves as human beings thoughtfully under construction realize their unfinishedness (or incompleteness, if one prefers), which, in turn, energizes their becoming, realizing their epistemological curiosities are driven by what they know and what they don't know in order to continue evolving, learning, growing, and changing (Kirylo 2011).

As one thoughtfully weaves through this purposeful and necessary reflective process, the importance of realizing the place of disposition comes into play, the chapter discussion that will be explored next.

NOTE

1. If one's personal philosophy of education does not resonate well with respect to the school's mission, a teacher has four options to consider: (1) s/he can respectively discuss the school's mission statement with the administration and other teachers and staff, working to modify or change the mission; (2) s/he can work within that philosophy, yet operate in such a way to subvert or even transcend the school's mission in her/his practice, with hopes of having an influencing effect on others; (3) s/he can work

to look for another teaching position that better suits her/his philosophy; or (4) s/he can accept the mission statement and compromise her/his personal philosophy of education.

THREE
The Decisive Relevance of Disposition
Reconciling the Private with the Public

> *There cannot be two sets of ethical principles, one for life in the school, and the other for life outside of the school. As conduct is one, so also the principles of conduct are one.*
>
> (Dewey 1909, 7)

Associated with such terms as "attitude," "mood," "temperament," and tendencies to act or think in a particular way (Merriam-Webster 2012), the decisive relevance of disposition and its association to teachers is not a new idea.

John Dewey (1933) critically underscored the importance of personal disposition, making clear that, while one may possess methodological knowledge and even have desire, this attitudinal or dispositional state is not enough. What is also needed is an "understanding of the forms and techniques that are the channels through which these attitudes operate to the best advantage" (30).

In other words, for particular suitable dispositions to manifest themselves in practice, Dewey further suggests those dispositions must be cultivated through an attitude of open-mindedness (i.e., considering multiple points of view and possibilities), whole-heartedness (i.e., an undivided heart in order to absorb what we learn; a genuine enthusiasm), and responsibility (i.e., taking into thoughtful consideration of one's beliefs and the consequences of those beliefs; to responsibly engage students in meaningful subject matter).

The focused cultivation of these three attitudes are integral, leading to what Dewey describes as a "habit of thinking" influencing the formation of character (Dewey 1933). The implication thusly is that the routine of habit in the context of thinking implies that habits are not some mindless rulings that direct us; rather, thought informs our habits as a way of being, thinking, and doing (Dewey 1983).

ATTITUDE AS AN ASPECT OF DISPOSITION

To be more precise, attitude, as an aspect of disposition, is not in itself what concretizes it; but rather attitude is the manifestation of action that illuminates disposition. For example, one can have a negative attitude about going to work on a particular day, but deliberately rise above that attitude and effectively carry on.

Conversely, one may have a positive attitude about going to work, but the attitude itself does not translate into production. Moreover, one may possess the attitude, knowledge, and skills to do a job, but lack the "habit of mind" to purposely do the job, implying a lack of cognizant intention to work toward a desired goal (Katz 1993a).

In short, attitude does not necessarily forecast behavior or action; rather intentionality, a thoughtful voluntary act of the will, does. In that light, therefore, dispositions can be viewed as voluntary conscious acts of behavior that tend to be frequently exhibited (Katz 1993b). To move toward that end, the habit of mind needed to appropriate behaviors and actions that are intentionally thoughtful and intelligent is a disciplined mind (Costa and Kallick 2000).

While calling for the necessity of a disciplined mind is a good way of putting it in order to appropriate desired dispositional patterns, Ritchhart and Perkins (2000) argue rather for the cultivation of mindfulness, which is a state in one's being where one feels a sense of control of one's life, guided by creativity, flexibility, information, memory, and retention. To that end, therefore, disposition is viewed as a psychological element comprised of three constituents: sensitivity (i.e., an awareness of and alertness to occasions for engaging in certain behavior), inclination (i.e., the motivation or habit toward carrying out a particular behavior), and ability (i.e., the capability of carrying out that behavior) (30).

The inference of the three components suggests that the mindfulness infused in one's disposition is the engine that propels behavior, parallel to the thinking that explains the idea of activating intentional habits of the mind. For the teacher, Lovewell (2012) would characterize this way of thinking and doing as mindful teaching, which emanates from a heart-centered approach (mindfulness is further discussed in chapter 7.)

RECONCILING THE PUBLIC AND PRIVATE

Carroll (2007) reminds us that those who enter the teaching profession each brings their own particular orientations that guide personal values, beliefs, ideals, and ideas that have been shaped by family, peers, religious persuasions, education, and a host of other influences. These orientations impact viewpoint, judgment, and action, having a natural effect on what kind of teacher one will be.

To be sure, personal orientations must be reflectively explored and thoughtfully arbitrated and perhaps even transcended with respect to professional thought, conduct, practice, or approach. To state another way, it is important that teachers examine what they think, how they think, what processes are involved in the thinking, what influences filter the thinking, and ultimately how what is thought about is manifested into action.

For example, in order to promote a classroom environment of equality, justice, fairness, and tolerance, it is essential that a teacher examines personal values, beliefs, and attitudes when it comes to concepts related to race, gender, language, expectations, and economic class.

That is, a teacher necessarily must engage with self to authentically reconcile what s/he thinks and does in her/his private life with what s/he thinks and does in her/his public life as an educator regarding concepts related to diversity. And the idea of authenticity in this sphere suggests that the conscious self acts true according to one's self-understanding and ethical "code," which one has freely constructed in order to foster meaning and purpose in life (Kirylo 2011).

To illustrate the point, if a teacher privately holds intolerant tendencies toward a particular ethnic group, possesses low expectations for girls in particular disciplines, or views those in poverty in a condescending way, s/he will be challenged in two distinct ways. First, s/he has to come to that place to recognize that the thinking s/he has constructed will naturally play a detrimental role in her/his work as a teacher, and second, s/he will need to grasp the courage to authentically reconstruct her/his ethical code of thinking, which dismisses or transcends detrimental tendencies in her/his thought.

Indeed, this intricate dynamic is an introspective process that willingly yields toward a dispositional stance that "includes an active desire to listen to more sides than one; to give heed to facts from whatever sources they come; to give full attention to alternative possibilities; to recognize the possibility of error even in the beliefs that are dearest to us . . . It requires troublesome work to undertake the alteration of old beliefs (Dewey 1933, 30).

From another point of view regarding this introspective process and its link between the private and the public is to consider the teacher who may, in fact, authentically hold private values and thoughts that embrace diversity, high expectations for all, and which do not negatively stratify students, but yet her/his public effort in classroom practice is ill-prepared. In this case, the teacher clearly has an obligation to authentically reconcile her/his private beliefs with better preparation.

Finally, as a third illustration, a teacher may conceptually understand the need to teach reading and writing in developmentally appropriate ways to captivate the interest of her/his students, but if s/he does not in some form regularly engage in reading and writing in her/his private life, her/his pedagogical approach will ultimately emerge as inauthentic in terms of enthusiasm, variety, and ultimate purpose.

Assuredly, within age-appropriate boundaries, it is good practice when teachers regularly share with their students what they are reading, perhaps even showing respective texts to the class. It is also good practice when teachers regularly read aloud to their students, and it is certainly fitting when sustained silent reading and writing among all in the classroom community is a regular part of the daily routine.

Mindful of the previously discussed Deweyan notions of open-mindedness, whole-heartedness, and responsibility, Dewey (1964a, 1916) also astutely reasons that education as a process of living implies that to grow is to thoughtfully be under construction, reflectively negotiating what we think, believe, and value, and how it translates into action.

This, therefore, means that a teacher—particularly when it comes to personal attitudes, values, and beliefs that will have a direct impact on the lives of students—necessarily needs to move away from thinking dualistically, which says the private can be compartmentalized from the public.

Rather, the suggested thinking here is that one works to harmonize the private with the public, a dispositional process that is continuously under construction in building an authentic self that works to meaningfully meet the needs of all students. In the final analysis, the refinement of one's disposition is clearly a dynamic that bridges attitudes, values, knowledge, and skills with effective teaching, involving a systematic process that engages teachers to grow in awareness in realizing the various contexts inherent in teaching and the variety of actions that are needed to advance student learning (Schussler, Stooksberry, and Bercaw 2010).

The following chapter thus advocates what is characterized as dispositions of significance that every teacher ought to possess in order to foster the likelihood of connecting with a diverse student population.

FOUR
Six Dispositions of Significance

So faith, hope, and love remain, these three; but the greatest of these is love.

(I Corinthians 13:13)

The desirable dispositions of a teacher can vary from context, setting, circumstance, student population, and the political, social, and religious landscape, making teaching what Eisner (2006) calls a custom job. For example, the way a teacher thinks, prepares, and acts relative to her/his pedagogical approach on a Cheyenne River Indian Reservation in the western part of the United States will differ from that of Tonawanda Indian Reservation in the northeast part of the country; will differ from working in the city of Chicago, Illinois; from that in Hays, Kansas; will differ from working in Los Angeles, California; from that in El Paso, Texas, and so on.

While there are natural dispositional differences that teachers must consider relative to setting, circumstance, and time, there are, however, foundational humanizing dispositions all teachers ought to possess. Characterized as dispositions of significance, which will be sketched below, are love, faith, hope, humility, compassion, and persistence.

LOVE

When one asserts that s/he wants to teach because "I love children," the suggestion is that s/he desires to engage in relationship with youngsters, including the establishing of relationships with the parents of students, colleagues, and with the community at large. This implies that a loving relationship entails dialogue (see chapter 8), devotion, and mutual respect, and that the idea of love is moved by a deliberate decision, which promises to nourish meaning and good for the other (Fromm 2006).

Mother Teresa (1983) aptly states, "love cannot remain by itself—it has no meaning" (75). In a somewhat analogous way, Freire (2005) declares, "loving is not enough; one must know how to love" (82). In order for love to thusly have meaning, it must not only be an authentic emanation from the heart, but it also must be demonstrated in meaningful purpose. In other words, teachers are those who not only ought to be joyful, serious, rigorous, and scientific in their practice, but also be those who emanate a love for the other within the very process of teaching (Freire 2005).

FAITH

Because of their eternal significance and even characterized as theological virtues, a discussion about love is necessarily linked to the concepts of faith and hope. The idea of faith is naturally associated with one's belief system often expressed in one's religion or spirituality. It is reasonable to assume that the authenticity of one's faith is determined through the manifestation of how one communicates, what is communicated, as well as in behaviors and actions. And while faith is naturally linked to things of the spirit and religious belief systems, there is also the idea of faith expressed in the context of possessing a fundamental faith in the human family, which is revealed in how we relate to one another.

In drawing from William Fowler's work, *Stages of Faith* and H. Richard Niebuhr's, *Radical Monotheism and Western Culture*, Purpel (1989) emphasizes the value of faith in the context of how we care, trust, and relate to one another. From his text, *Does Civilization Need Religion?*, Niebuhr (1927) succinctly puts it this way: "Men [and women] cannot create a society if they do not believe in each other" (62).

To state another way, because education is an endeavor that works to change lives, it is a journey to become more fully human, which is only possible in relationships, markedly exemplified by adopting "an article of faith" that believes in the betterment of the other (Ayers 2005). Indeed, for the teacher, the "other," in particular, is the student who stands right before her/him.

HOPE

While hope is a concept that is viewed as a theological virtue, it is also, however, a necessary psychological element that provides for human beings a sense of purpose in order to live meaningfully. As Komonchak, Collins, and Lane (1987) put it, "hope is the presupposition behind the human 'will to live'" (493). The antithesis of hope is hopelessness, which debilitates because it immobilizes, distorts, and sees reality as deterministic with no possibility of change (Freire 1998a).

Therefore, for teachers, hope is not some abstract concept; it is concretized when they realize its powerful mobilizing agency not only in their own lives, but also in the lives of their students. To the latter, hope manifests itself in respectful communication and meaningful interaction, in the giving of time, in steadfast encouragement, in the power of stirring imaginations, in the sincere belief that change is possible, and in the belief of possibilities for the other.

HUMILITY

In the higher and admirable sense of the word, humility describes one as modest, unassuming, and unpretentious. From a spiritual perspective, the characteristic of humility genuinely places ego to the side, allowing one to authentically yield and to be open to God (or the transcendent), others, and to grow in wisdom. In other words, as Nouwen (1983) asserts, "it [humility] means staying close to the ground (*humus*), to people, to everyday life, to what is happening with all its down-to-earthness. It is the virtue that opens our eyes for the presence of God on the earth" (162).[1]

Thus, humility necessitates a letting go of preconceived notions of what is, who we are, and perhaps even who God is. Mother Teresa (1996) suggests that the reality of truth cannot be spoken without simultaneously considering the value and necessity of humility. In that light, Freire (2005) makes the point, "humility helps us to understand this obvious truth: No one knows it all; no one is ignorant of everything. We all know something; we are all ignorant of something . . . Humility helps me avoid being entrenched in the circuit of my own truth" (72).

Hence, in the act of teaching, one is also in the primal position to learn from students, implying a profound respect for those students and taking the time to listen to them. In other words, a dispositional stance of humility opens wide the avenue for teachers to intimately connect with their students. Palmer (1993), in his work *To Know as We Are Known*, insightfully explains:

> Humility is the virtue that allows us to pay attention to "the other"—be it student or subject—whose integrity and voice are so central to knowing and teaching in truth . . . Humility not only creates a space in which the other can speak; it also allows to enter into obedience to the other . . . In humility we allow ourselves to know and be known in relationship, and in that allowing we draw our students into the community of truth. (108–09)

While humility, as described above, is demonstrated through modest behavior, keeping one close to the ground, guides the certainty-uncertainty tension of our truth, and is critical in fostering connection with students; it does not imply, however, a resignation, weakness, or disregard for oneself; in fact, humility is an act of courage and indicative of self-confidence (Freire 2005).

Stated another way, humility is the ability to:

- Admit limitations and weaknesses, leading to a clearer understanding of oneself;
- Thoughtfully discern biases and prejudices, leading to tolerance, acceptance, understanding, and empathy;
- Recognize and determine that one's lens of the world may quite possibly be too narrow and limiting, leading to a more holistic perspective;
- Admit that one may not be as informed as s/he ought, leading to a pursuit of knowledge and information;
- Discern a healthy ego as opposed to being egotistical;
- Get in touch with and constructively address what Carl Jung calls our shadow—that is, those areas in our lives that, in large part, are associated with negativity, insecurity, and discomfort; and
- Accept individual strength, insight, knowledge, wisdom, and intelligence as gifts that are to be nurtured, refined, and ultimately used as a service to others.

COMPASSION

Compassion, which is intricately linked to the qualities of empathy and care, comes from the Latin *compati*, meaning to be conscious and aware of another's difficulty and distress while simultaneously seeking out possible solutions and alternatives to alleviate anxiety and troubles.

Therefore, as it relates to the concept of care, Mayeroff (1971) makes the point that the idea of caring is not an abstract concept, or a momentary event, but rather a way of relating with another. In other words, the process of caring aids in facilitating growth, relationship, and especially illuminates itself in realizing another's potential, possibilities, particularly when facing obstacles and times of difficulty.

The motivation that drives caring actions assumes a stepping out of self, out of one's frame of reference in order to consider the point of view, objective needs, and welfare of the other (Noddings 2013). For teachers, this can be manifested in the way they model caring in their relationships with students (even with the parents of students and colleagues), how they engage students in dialogue, and how they create opportunities that are purposeful, which fosters caring and confirms the better self in students (Noddings 1992; Pugach 2006).

Mayeroff (1971) further posits the following eight major elements that comprise caring: *knowing* (knowing the other; aware of how to respond to their needs); *alternative rhythms* (in tune with the usefulness and value of caring actions, modifying where necessary); *patience* (enabling and believing in the growth of the other in its own time); *honesty* (being received as true and authentic, and truly seeing the other as is); *trust* (through encouragement, assistance, and letting go, allowing the space for the other to grow, to learn from mistakes, and to find their own way); *humility* (as discussed above, to learn from the other, and mutually learn); *hope* (as also alluded to above, genuinely realizes the potential for the other, cultivating the present while anticipating future possibilities); and *courage* (moving forward to the unknown, with no guarantees, trusting in the care given and the growth of the other).

While the above eight elements of caring provide rich food for thought in which compassion is naturally linked, the action of caring is not formulistic or rule-bound, but rather a way of being, a pattern of living that responds to the moment, to the event, to life itself (Noddings 2013, 1992; Pugach 2006; Mayeroff 1971).

PERSISTENCE

A synonym for the word "persistence" is "perseverance," which implies maintaining a steadfast stance within the midst of facing obstacles, challenges, competing thoughts, emotions, and feelings. For the teacher, therefore, being persistent suggests that, despite the odds, circumstances, situations, and multiple other factors, because *every* child is unique and specially created, the teacher remains resolute in believing in the possibilities of each child.

The other side of the coin of persistence in upholding its resolve is consistency (also see chapter 18). When teachers exude a persistent-consistent resolve pattern, students are provided with a grounded understanding of who their teachers are and where they are coming from, which nurtures a predictable regularity in a classroom setting, providing the integral sustenance of a teacher's words and action (LaCaze and Kirylo 2012).

Most certainly, however, a teacher's patience level will barometrically be tested in her/his practice in the effort to maintain that persistence-consistent resolve pattern. In other words, a classroom teacher generally works with children from diverse backgrounds, various personalities, and at times interacts with students and families who, for a number of reasons, are challenging or difficult.

And perhaps in a moment of exasperation during one of those challenging episodes while working with one of her/his difficult students, a well-meaning teacher may find herself uttering the statement "you can't save them all." While there may be an understandable job-coping-mechanism aspect of that pronouncement, it is, however, a paving of the road toward the abdication of responsibility for two fundamental reasons.

First, when teachers begin to embrace the concept "I can't save them all," they are opening the proverbial crack in the door toward pedagogical shut-down, which only adds to the intensity of the conflict, simply because this viewpoint offers no direction, no movement toward solutions.

Of course, it would be nice if there were a magic answer, an immediate solution, or a strategic pedagogical formula that was guaranteed. But there is not, and rarely is for a teacher. In short, an "I can't save them all" position can easily translate into—at best—only peripherally working with the challenging student with low expectations in mind; and—at worst—giving up on the child with no expectations at all.

Second, the task of the teacher is not to "save" a child. Rather, the fundamental task of the teacher is three-fold: (a) to engage in an instructional practice that is developmentally appropriate in order to make connections with a child so that meaningful learning can take place; (b) to deeply understand that working with challenging children obviously does not mean acceptance of disruption, inappropriate behavior, or noncompliance. It means, however, to authentically exhaust every effort to find solutions and seek appropriate ways to constructively deal with them; and (c) to thoughtfully reflect on one's practice. The depth of the latter determines the degree of insightfulness and innovation of the former (a concept explored in the next chapter).

In the end, when working with a challenging student, the notion of "can't" should not enter into the lexicon. What enters the mind and action of the teacher is concepts such as "persistence," "belief," "will," and "connection." The idea of being persistent is thus a way of being and a way of acting in order to move, prod, and suggest, paving the way toward tapping into the unique gifts, strengths, and talents of each student. To state differently, persistence is a key ingredient in instilling high expectations, playing a critical role in fostering reflection of practice, in overcoming difficulties, having a positive impact on teacher efficacy, and cultivating excellence in teaching practice (Wheatley n.d.).

On its surface, these six dispositions of significance (love, faith, hope, humility, compassion, and persistence) appear straightforward to conceptually grasp, but clearly in the profundity of their depth and breadth, the idea of moving these dispositions as mindful habits of thought and action is a continuous inner process that is rooted in a personal philosophy of education and propelled through the dialectical interweaving of reflection and action, which will be explored in the final chapter of this section.

NOTE

1. While there is a certain synergy between humility and belief in God, a higher power, or a transcendent entity, the notion of humility is obviously not solely confined with its link to otherworldliness. It indeed is a prolific human virtue that greatly works to illuminate the goodness, kindness, and "humanness" of what it means to be human.

FIVE

Reflective Thinking— Thoughtful Action

Reflection is essential for growth, development, and change. It is the unique power of the human person.

(Nouwen 1996, 27)

Thinking that is reflective is more than whatever stream of thought may be flowing through one's mind; rather, reflective thought—which frees one from acting on impulse or thoughtless routine—enables thoughtful action that is conducted with deliberate purpose. Moreover, reflective thought embraces the critical space of doubt, hesitation, and perplexity within the act of pensively searching and inquiring in order to come to some kind of resolution to settle that doubt (Dewey 1933). In other words, *"active, persistent, and careful consideration of any belief or supposed form of knowledge in the light of the grounds that support it and the further conclusions to which it tends* constitutes reflective thought (Dewey 1933, 9, author's emphasis).

In interpreting Dewey's idea and purpose of reflection, Rodgers (2002) emphasizes that reflection is a process that is systematic and disciplined, values personal and intellectual development of oneself and of the other, occurs in community, and is a meaning-making process that is threaded through the connecting of experiences and ideas as a means to some moral end. To be sure, the reflective process is a distinct way of thinking and requires practice, requiring:

> The teacher to confront the complexity of students and their learning, of themselves and their teaching, their subject matter, and the contexts in which all these operate. Any action the teacher takes, therefore, will be considered rather than impulsive and based on a deep knowledge of

each of these elements and their interactions, which ultimately can only benefit students' learning. (Rodgers 2002, 864)

Not allowing for one to stay stuck on "automatic pilot," reflection and its association to practice challenges one to dig deep about what s/he thinks, how information is filtered, how and what s/he communicates, and how s/he processes decisions (Sparks-Langer and Colton 1991; Barone 1983).

Teachers who thoughtfully engage in reflecting on their practice are those who can be characterized as reflective practitioners, making the ongoing conscious decision to contextually examine their pedagogical practice and the everyday decisions they make. And an important natural underlying assumption within this reflective practitioner stance is that the teacher is one who keeps up professionally. Indeed, there is a positive correlation with those who keep up professionally and maintain an effective instructional practice (Darling-Hammond 1997); moreover, self-improvement is the "mark of a professional" (Henderson and Hawthorne 2000, 67).

Recognizing, therefore, the critical importance of examining experience, the context of that experience, and the cyclical nature of the thought and action process, the teacher is thus more of a creative artist/designer as opposed to an engineer/technician, all of which plays a significant role in reminding the teacher that her/his work is about service to the other as opposed to serving a system (Wellington 1991).

Furthermore, a reflective practitioner is one who is positioned in a *knowing-in-action* stance (the tacit knowledge of one's practice is evident in practice), which then continues to be refined through a thoughtful process that engages in *reflection-in-action* (as a regular discipline of simultaneously reflecting and making adjustments during one's practice), and *reflection-on-action* (as a regular discipline of looking back to critically examine the results, outcomes, and consequences of one's practice) (Schön 1983, 1987).

Drawing from rational and intuitive thought, and assuming one possesses the skills and inclination, the process involved in reflective thinking indeed is a systematic dynamic seeking to analyze a problem, an idea, or an event. And the assumption guiding this reflective process presumes the earlier discussed Deweyan concepts (see chapter 3) in which teacher attitude is guided by open-mindedness, responsibility, and wholeheartedness (LaBoskey 1994).

MORE THAN A METHODOLOGICAL UNDERTAKING

Illuminated by the dispositions of significance, cognizant of one's unfinishedness, possessing a recognition that education is about entering into diverse relationships (see section II), aware of the illuminating power of inspiration and the artistry of teaching (see section III), informed with an adept grasp of educational psychology and the five components of teacher knowledge (see sections IV and V), having a clear understanding of the place and purpose of assessment (see section VI), and realizing what it means to be a teacher leader (see section VII)—engaging in reflective practice is not for the shallow, but rather for the dedicated as a way of being, as a "habit" of mind that energizes and critically drives what it means to teach with purpose.

In fact, because teaching is more than a methodological undertaking, the idea of teaching effectively without a commitment to reflective practice is not an option. And perhaps paradoxically, this commitment is not one that ought to be conducted out of compulsion, but rather it is one that is naturally embraced by those who care to contextually and insightfully teach.

While there is no formula (nor should there be) on what it takes to move toward being a reflective practitioner, there are a few broad practices that all teachers can do to work toward that end:

- As underscored in chapter 2, critically reflect, discuss, and read about what you epistemologically, ontologically, and axiologically believe, mindful that this is an ongoing dialectical process in which thought informs practice and practice informs thought.
- As also underscored in chapter 2, develop a personal philosophy of education (which likely may need revision from time to time). Be ready to articulate your philosophy when asked and visibly display it in the classroom. Perhaps keep in mind three talking bulleted points that succinctly articulate your philosophy.
- Be able to thoughtfully respond as to why you want to be a teacher, perhaps in three bulleted talking points (as in the case with the above).
- Journal regularly (even if it is only for five minutes daily), reflecting on teaching dilemmas, challenges, and pleasures you face daily. As in the process in the first bulleted point, the ongoing dialectical process of journaling aids greatly in informing thought, and thought greatly informs action, leading back to informing thought.
- Regularly read from a variety of writers who aid in fostering thinking, reflection, and discovery. Again, as in the journaling process, this reading process informs thought, and thought informs action.
- Associate with others who demonstrate a pedagogical practice that is thoughtful, developmentally appropriate, and just. Remaining in regular conversations with like-minded individuals supports greatly in our continuous striving toward excellence.
- Regularly meditate, have moments of silence, which will greatly assist in remaining grounded on the everlasting things of life (i.e., love, hope, and faith).

- Maintain an attitude that is open to other points of view, other ways of thinking, and different ways of doing.
- Learn to transcend negative attitudes.
- Admit to limitations and weaknesses in order to move toward constructiveness and correction.
- Affirm personal strengths, gifts, and talents.
- Maintain a healthy diet and regular exercise.
- Be in the moment when teaching (i.e., remain steadfastly thoughtful in processing all pedagogical decisions, and work to be mindfully present in every interaction).

In the final analysis, the twine that works to strongly weave thought, knowledge, and action is the dialectical process of reflective practice. The more teachers engage in this process, the more likelihood they thoughtfully know who they are, what informs their practice, and how they meaningfully interact with their students. Teachers who engage in reflective practice realize that they ultimately teach who they are, yet realizing that teaching is not about "me," but rather about the other.

To put another way, teaching is not about me because *I* responded to the "call," and because it makes *me* feel good (although that is a natural consequence); rather, teaching is about what one's students are experiencing, what opportunities they are given, and how they are viewed, treated, and valued. In short, the transformative dynamic of reflective practice has energizing, life-changing implications, necessarily guiding an inner accountability relative to one's relationships, work, effort, and vision as a teacher.

Section II

Entering into Relationships

The direction to the right pew in education—like the real estate mantra of location, location, location—is relationships, relationships, relationships.

(Comer 2004, 2)

SIX
Hardwired to Be in Relationships

A Thing of the Brain

>*Relationships that are "connecting" and allow for collaboration appear to offer children a wealth of interpersonal closeness that supports the development of many domains, including social, emotional, and cognitive functioning.*
>
> (Siegel 2001, 78)

An understanding that places meaning in our existence is to be aware that there is a today, a tomorrow, a yesterday, a past, present, and future. Moreover, as human beings we are more than able to act on instinct, able to transcend impulse; we possess the capacity to ethically, morally, spiritually, intellectually, and physically think through dilemmas, conflicts, and challenges; and we can somehow sort through the meaning of love, friendship, and relationships of all stripes. Particularly with respect to the latter, we are predisposed to be in relationships. Or, as A. Banks (2010) indicates, we are hardwired to connect, suggesting that neuroscience confirms that the nervous system is "wired" for human beings to connect with one another.

Neuroscience intersects the disciplines of biology, chemistry, physics, mathematics, and the computer sciences in studying the operations of the nervous system of all life forms. The fusion of neuroscience, developmental psychology (the study of physical, psychological, and cognitive growth in human beings), and psychiatry (medical specialty treating mental disorders) presents a neurobiology of interpersonal experience, which is essentially driven by the following assumptions (Siegel 1999, 2):

- The human mind emerges from patterns in the flow of energy and information within the brain and between brains.

- The mind is created within the interaction of internal neurophysiological processes and interpersonal experiences.
- The structure and function of the developing brain are determined by how experiences, especially within interpersonal relationships, shape the genetically programmed maturation of the nervous system.

The brain, the central organ in the nervous system, is comprised of three broad parts: the cerebrum (largest part of the brain, filling much of the skull, involved in movement, feeling, thinking, problem solving, and remembering, critically integrating all forms of information); cerebellum (sitting under the cerebrum at the back of the head, involved in motor functions such as balance and movement); and the brainstem (located caudally, meaning toward the tail of the cerebrum, which is that part of the brain involved in autonomic functions such as cardiovascular regulation, i.e., heart rate and blood pressure and respiratory regulation, i.e., breathing) (Siegel 2001, 1999).

The brain consists of approximately one hundred billion neurons, which are the excitable nerve cells within the nervous system that process and transmit electrical signals (also referred to as action potentials) to, from, and within the brain. The connection between neurons (each neuron on average is connected to ten thousand other neurons) signal to each other by sending an electrical impulse through long axons, which then transport a neurotransmitter through synapses, all at rates up to two hundred miles per hour (Siegel 2001, 1999).

Each neuron, on average, has one thousand synaptic endings, implying an estimated quadrillion connections between the one hundred billion neurons. Jointly, the number of neurons that comprise the brain would stretch to a length of over two million miles, clearly making this dynamic living structure with its interconnected sections (parts), the most extraordinarily complex system known to humankind (Siegel 2001, 1999).

The brain is the most undifferentiated matter of the body at birth, implying that genetic makeup and the initiation of experience impact the profile of neural connection, forming a specific movement that assists in steering the emergence of mental development (Siegel 1999). To put it another way, particularly crucial at a young age between the parent–child relationship, interpersonal experiences impact the shape of neuron connection, influencing the uncovering of the mind (Siegel 2001, 1999).

And the mind, an abstract conception, yet one that is disclosed as a result of the brain's activity through interpersonal interactions, is that part of humanity that explains the conscious self, enabling thinking, feeling, awareness, judgment, understanding, and reason. In short, the mind materializes as a result of the activity that occurs in the brain, meaning experiences are what trigger the brain's neural pathways, which creates new connections and strengthens existing ones (Siegel 2001, 1999).

DEVELOPMENT OF THE MIND

What the above tells us is that the development of the mind occurs through the convergence of neurophysiological processes and interpersonal relationships. In other words, as Siegel (1999) puts it:

> Relationship experiences have a dominant influence on the brain because the circuits responsible for social perception are the same as or tightly linked to those that integrate the important functions controlling the creation of meaning, the regulation of bodily states, the modulation of emotion, the organization of memory, and the capacity for interpersonal communication. Interpersonal experience thus plays a special organizing role in determining the development of brain structure early in life and the ongoing emergence of brain function throughout the lifespan. (21)

The notion that interpersonal experience plays a lifelong continuous role in brain development implies that the plasticity of the brain, referred to as the science of neuroplasticity, allows for the brain to be continuously enabled for "neurons and neural networks to be born, grow, and change the way they relate to one another in response to experience" (Cozolino 2013, 159).[1]

To be sure, this is no small matter, for at one time, it was thought that the brain was imbued with a fixed amount of cells, and once cells died for a variety of reasons (age, head trauma, alcohol consumption, depression, abuse, neglect, etc.), the brain was on a no-reversal-trajectory toward gradual deterioration. However, we now know that the brain is able to "rewire" itself and produce new cells, particularly energized by meaningful relationships (A. Banks 2010).

Indeed, the operative here is centered on *meaningful*, in order that the plasticity of the brain is optimized for neural connection. That is, on the one hand, relational environments that are stressful, tension-filled, and nonstimulating negatively impact plasticity, growth, and learning. On the other hand, however, relationships that are meaningfully situated in a secure, trustworthy, emotional, socially, cognitive and physically supportive environment can shape neuroplastic activity toward growth and learning (Cozolino 2013; Siegel 2013; A. Banks 2010).

It can be said, therefore, that the brain is a social organ intricately linked to other brains, and the regulation impacting the brain's ability to learn is associated with how we treat and communicate with one another (even as it relates to eye contact, physical contact, and expressions), naturally having great implications for the classroom teacher (Cozolino 2013). As Siegel (2013) puts it, "teachers are the experiential sculptors who facilitate environments for students to become receptive, shaping the brains of our next generation of learners" (xii).

In the final analysis, the nurturing of relationships is foundationally a "brain thing," suggesting, as will be discussed in the next chapter, that the building of meaningful relationships at a school setting richly feeds the brain in maximizing the likelihood of learning, growth, harmony, and the building of the collective community.

NOTE

1. To explain differently, this "plasticity" in the brain is an activity in which synapses (connections between neurons) can and do change all the time, which happens on time scales of milliseconds to seconds to minutes to hours to years to a lifetime.

SEVEN

Fostering the Teacher–Student Relationship

From Right Where They Are

> *Relationships are at the heart of educational encounters . . . It is critically important that educators become more attentive to how their relationship is with their students individually and collectively.*
>
> (Giles, Smythe, and Spence 2012, 215–33)

A child psychiatrist and the founding member of the Comer School Development Program, James P. Comer has been extraordinarily influential in shaping educational thought, particularly underscoring the intimate connection between development and learning.

Among other domains of child and adolescent development, Comer emphasizes a developmental focus on the physical, cognitive, language, social, ethical, and psychological, which is maximally fostered in a learning environment that is integrative and holistic. And the thread that purposely links the developmental with meaningful learning is the establishment of authentic relationships between the teacher and student. Indeed, a foundational mantra of what schooling is about is relationships, relationships, relationships (Comer 2004).[1]

According to Merriam-Webster (2012), a definition of relationship refers to the way people behave, talk, and deal with one another. A teacher fundamentally enters into relationship patterns that can broadly fall into four distinct categories: between the student and the teacher; between the parent and the teacher; between the teacher and her colleagues; and between the teacher and the wider community.

The question, therefore, is what are the attributes needed by teachers in order to appreciatively behave, talk, and deal with the various relationships they enter into as educators? While each of these relationship patterns is distinctly nuanced and each will be discussed, the primary emphasis underscored in section II focuses on fostering the student–teacher relationship.

STUDENTS COME JUST AS THEY ARE

Through the influence of their lived reality, family, friends, neighbors, and a variety of others, a child enters school with his/her brain fashioned by the relationships that have early on been established.

This, of course, implies students come to the classroom setting with a variety of dispositional and attitudinal stances, with some more prepared than others; some more active than others; some more curious than others; some more quiet than others; some needing more attention than others; some more withdrawn than others; some more outgoing than others; some more attentive than others; and some hungry, tired, frightened, happy, bright-eyed, and ready.

Additionally, students arrive to the classroom door representing a variety of cultural influences, races, ethnicities, languages, economic classes, and family structures. In that light, therefore, the building of meaningful relationships between the teacher and student is highly dependent on the initiative taken by the teacher once the student enters the classroom door. That is, the teacher should work from a proactive (i.e., taking initiative, anticipatory attentive action) and prosocial (i.e., respectful, wellbeing of the other, caring) place, understanding that students enter the classroom door "just as they are."

In short, students come through those classroom doors not as some preconceived abstract idea of who the teacher thinks they are or ought to be; but, rather, students come through those doors as individual human beings predisposed to entering into relationship from right where they are.

What is being suggested is that the teacher enter into an I–thou relationship pattern, a concept originating from Martin Buber (1878–1965). In his classic book *I and Thou*, Buber (1958) emphasizes that the I–thou relationship is fundamental to engage in the human experience as opposed to an I–it relationship pattern. The former is driven by the notion of authentic dialogue, implying a coexisting relationship between persons; the latter is propelled by the idea that the I is the creator of things and the manipulator of the other. The idea of an "it" in the context of relationships views the other as an object, not only subverting the fostering of dialogue, but also represents a deformation of education (Freire 1994b).

In the context of education, therefore, the idea of the unfolding of an I–thou relationship functions through a teacher's ability to be available and present with her students. That is, the I and the thou suggests we are not alone; we coexist; there is a between with one to another, all of which is an encounter of inclusion. And this encounter is fostered by an environment that is mindfully dialogical (Woo 2012). Ayers (1993) frames it the following way:

> Teaching is a human activity, constrained and made possible by all the limits and potential that characterize any other human activity. Teaching depends on people—people who choose to teach and other people who become students by choice or not. There are these two sides to teaching, and on each side there are human beings, whole people with their own unique thoughts, hopes, dreams, aspirations, needs, experiences, contexts, agendas, and priorities. Teaching is relational and interactive. It requires dialogue, give and take, back and forth. It is multi-directional. This explains in part why every teaching encounter is particular, each unique in its details. (16)

The multidirectional trajectory of the variety of unique encounters the teacher faces is nourished by recognizing individual identities and mentalities (Gutiérrez, 1990), realizing that meaningful communication is what fosters an education of truth where "the teacher's thinking is authenticated only by the authenticity of the student's thinking" (Freire 1990, 63–64).

MINDFULNESS

The idea of authenticating a student's thinking is to be in that place of mindfulness. Building on the concept that was introduced in chapter 3, the cultivation of mindfulness by the teacher is one who recognizes the importance of nonjudgmental presence in the moment, to savor the experience, and to be aware of the nuances of activity (Ponton 2012; Johnson 2001).

The practice of mindfulness in action is optimized by a mindsight way of thinking, which means one is deeply aware of one's internal world, enabling an attentive monitoring system that keenly gauges one's thoughts, feelings, and motives. This monitoring dynamic not only allows one to be an active participant in life, but also greatly provides the mechanism to thoughtfully steer an interaction with the other that is empathetic, compassionate, and considerate (Siegel n.d.).

Arguing that mindfulness is at the core of nourishing relationships and mindsight is the capability to deeply perceive, focus, and see, Siegel and Hartzell (2003), in their text *Parenting from the Inside Out*, contend that a parent living in the moment not only assists in an awareness of thinking and feeling occurring in self, but also opens one up to be aware of those of their children. To that end, clarity and presence of self allows for appreciating difference, realizing the importance of recognizing individual experience, that no two individuals view things in the precise same manner, and to render "respect to the sovereignty of each person's unique mind" (Siegel and Hartzell 2003, 7).

The implications for the classroom teacher are four-fold: first, an undistracted manner of communication that is purposeful, mentally present, and intentional validates the presence of the individual student, their experience, their sense of self. Second, a manner of communication that is focused looks beyond the superficial level of behaviors, actions, and inactions of students, and goes deeper in seeking for an understanding of the motivation and the why of those behaviors. Third, not only are words and tone critical in what is communicated, but also awareness of the signals being sent through nonverbal cues such as eye contact, posture, and expression are essential in understanding how one communicates. Finally, in a dialogical environment (the theme of the next chapter), both teacher and student learn and grow together (Siegel and Hartzell 2003).

NOTE

1. http://www.schooldevelopmentprogram.org/about/development.aspx.

EIGHT
Cultivating Dialogue

Dialogue is thus an existential necessity . . . Dialogue cannot exist, however, in the absence of a profound love for the world.

(Freire 1990, 77)

The idea of dialogue is not simply a "conversation" as one can find in a contemporary dictionary definition of the term, suggesting that it (dialogue) is merely a sharing of ideas. Moreover, dialogue is more than the Socratic notion of it, when Socrates utilizes it as a teaching tool in order for subjects to rediscover forgotten ideas or knowledge. Rather, dialogue, as an element that is nourished by truth, is a humanizing mechanism that encourages democratic participation, honoring individual spoken realities in order to learn, understand, and transform (Collins 1977; Freire 1990, 1985). In order to better appreciate the point, it is worth recalling the derivative of dialogue and clarifying the distinct difference between dialogue and monologue.

"Dialogue" is a term that is derived from the Greek, *dia*, which signifies across or through, and *logue*, derived from *logos* (word), meaning speech, conversation or discourse. Also, as the Greek derivative suggests, dialogue implies an exchange between two individuals (or groups/entities), which is obviously different than the notion of a monologue. The latter, with its prefix *mono*, Greek for single or alone, implies that there is no discourse or exchange involved; only one person (or group/entity) speaks. In other words, monologue has no concern with ascertaining a response.

Dialogue, however, with its root implication of "coming across" or "getting through," assumes that within the exchange of the word there is another side, another story, another point of view that, respectively, needs to be considered. In short, key to a dialogical relationship is authentic listening (Freire 1997), a point that will be further discussed later.

In a school setting, the beginning point of a dialogical relationship, therefore, not only assumes the learner possesses distinct value, but also presupposes that schooling is a dynamic that involves the psychological, cultural, and experiential level of the learner (Freire 1994b). Moreover, it assumes that the relationship between the educator and the learner is not one of a hierarchal top-down paradigm or one that is of a vertical nature, which is played out through an antidialogue stance that is not concerned about another point of view; its only concern is its own content, its own point of view, and its own subjugation (Freire 1990).

Rather, authentic dialogue fosters a horizontal relationship between educator and learner, which impacts the building of trust, through which the dialogical occurrence begins with the learner as the subject engaged in a process whereby s/he plays an integral role as creator and maker of the world (Freire 1994b). To put another way, as Noddings (1992) declares, "Dialogue is a common search for understanding, empathy, and appreciation. It can be playful or serious, logical or imaginative, goal or process orientated, but it is always a genuine quest for something at the beginning" (23).

Particularly with respect to considering the object of study, the quest of the dialogical setting contains a certain purpose and structure that steers the engagement of the study (Roberts 2010; Shor and Freire 1987). In other words, for dialogue to be a critical aspect of meaningful learning, it is more than a casual conversation among friends who are not necessarily discussing the delimitations of an identified object; rather, dialogue is an epistemological endeavor whereby the educator maintains his/her epistemological curiosity, while at the same time cultivating critical reflection in a process through which dialogical spaces are created in order that students are apprenticed in the necessary thoroughness involved in exploration (Freire and Macedo, 1995). Palmer (1993) puts it this way, explaining "that real learning does not happen until students are brought into relationship with the teacher, with each other, and with the subject. We cannot learn deeply and well until a community of learning is created in the classroom" (xvi).

In the end, the move toward dialogue is what makes us uniquely human, and for it to be transformative, the presence of love (suggesting a commitment to others), humility (suggesting not to act in arrogance and to recognize the other), hope (grounding our incompleteness in the search for meaning), faith in humanity (believing in the power of human beings toward the building of a more humanized world), and critical thinking (enabling dialogue to exist in a discerning way)—are all necessary aspects of a dialogical relationship (Freire 1990). Clearly, the fostering of dialogue is the cornerstone of building enduring relationships, and listening is the heart that propels its substance.

THE HEART OF DIALOGUE: LISTENING

A few years ago, Seth S. Horowitz, an auditory neuroscientist, wrote a *Sunday Review* opinion piece for the *New York Times* titled "The Science and Art of Listening," where he describes the interrelated dynamic of hearing and listening. As a process in the brain, through development and experience, hearing can be characterized as our finely tuned alarm system that remains in perpetual autopilot, enabling a "volume control" that regulates the ability for one to "tune in" or "tune out" most sounds (other than those that acutely signal danger or something delightful).

For example, one can choose to tune out the slight whirring sound of a computer or can choose to be attentive to its sound. And if one decides on the latter, the brain is ignited to direct the sensory event by consciously paying attention to the whirring sound of the computer. What this translates to, when it comes to relationships, is that hearing and the enacting of listening is enabled to the degree one pays attention to the other (Horowitz 2012). In short, the skill of listening is driven by attentiveness.

The posture of one's mind with respect to undistracted focus, the body language, facial expressions, and eye contact that radiates welcome, and the quality of time given to the other are key in conveying listening with attentiveness. Students tend to grow in trust and be more open to their teacher when it is apparent to them that their teacher genuinely listens without putting them under the scrutiny of judgment and evaluation for what they are communicating (Eggen and Kauchak 2004).

Further making the point, Deiro (1997) reasons, "the more time one spends with another, the more one has the opportunity to know and trust the other . . . The more time a teacher spends with a student showing caring and concern for that student, the more that student will develop feelings of closeness and trust with that teacher" (196).[1] In short, maximum attention and responding to the emotional and intellectual substance of the messages communicated by the student is what marks active listening (Eggen and Kauchak 2004).

In the final analysis, by actively listening to students (and the parents/caregivers of students) with focused attention, teachers have the opportunity to do the following:

- Capture a glimpse of their world, which leads them to be more empathetic with various student struggles;
- Have the opportunity to validate what students (and parents/caregivers) say as important, which leads to a better understanding of who they are and how they can teach for individual differences;
- Can garner information about individual students, which may be quite instrumental, leading to a cultivation of student self-affirmation;
- Are able to step back, leading to reflection; and

- Finally, begin the first move of valuing the other; begin the first step of entering into dialogue.

And with respect to dialogue, this critical step is one which permeates with the flow of integrity, the theme of the next chapter.

NOTE

1. With respect to large classes, which is often the case, Deiro (1997) makes clear the challenge involved in an effort to carve out quality time to individually interact with students, emphasizing it is a commitment that nurturing teachers have made through a variety of ways, such as making it a point to daily greet students at the doorway, and similarly at the same station bid farewell at the end of the day. Moreover, these same teachers make themselves available between classes, before and after school, get involved with extracurricular activities, and facilitate openness to students if they want to discuss anything that is pressing their mind. Finally, nurturing teachers will attempt to coordinate class activities divided up in small groups, providing a more manageable means for teachers to qualitatively interact with students; will interject personal experiences within their instructional approach, displaying a sense of vulnerability and approachability to their students; and will show personal interest through the writing of notes on their papers before handing them back.

NINE
The Flow of Integrity

Integrity largely has to do with purifying our intentions.

(Rohr 2011, xv)

Integrity, derived from the Latin *integritatem*, signifies wholeness, soundness, and blamelessness. These qualities are exemplified by a moral order that is manifested in a consistency of honesty, justice, and principled ways of acting and doing. With respect to relationships, the flow of integrity functions through dialogue, mindful that listening is the heart that attains the authenticity of dialogue, all of which is tightly threaded through the virtuousness of trust and respect.

BUILDING TRUST

The building of trust has no room for pretense, but rather is shaped by an environment that is genuine in the way people communicate with one another. In its essence, trust involves the cognitive, emotional, and behavioral aspects of being, allowing for the possibilities for human interactions to function in a space of simplicity and confidence (Lewis and Weigert 1985). As a socially constructed phenomenon, therefore, the dynamic of trust bonds relationships (Weber and Carter 1998), distinctively evident in those that manifest attributes related to openness, benevolence, honesty, reliability, competence, and vulnerability (Dumford 2010; Lewis 2008).

As a teacher consistently exhibits a temperament of those aforementioned attributes, students are provided with a sense of security and empowerment in building their level of confidence and awareness of voice, realizing that learning unfolds through an exploration of ideas and concepts. In other words, in a space of trust, students are more apt "to put themselves out there" in demonstrating what they know, don't know, and what they still need to learn, moving toward an understanding that schooling is not simply about a grade, but about learning. To be sure, the notion of this dynamic places students in a place of vulnerability, not only in front of the teacher, but also those of their peers (Durnford 2010). Moreover, the fostering of a trusting environment enables students to realize the reciprocation involved in the process, which impacts the nurturing of mutual respect, understanding, and expectations (Durnford 2010; Weber and Carter 1998).

Indeed, a teacher's credibility is greatly heightened when students (and their parents/caregivers) come to recognize that the teacher genuinely has their overall best interest in mind, particularly manifested in the teacher's competence, reliability, level of fairness, and thoughtful communication, all of which facilitates a bond of trust, and better positions students toward success. In the end, the idea of gaining trust is not a singular event, but rather a process that evolves over time, which is necessarily sustained through the consistency of words and actions (Durnford 2010; Weber and Carter 1998).

The nature of trust and the evolving process that it takes to appropriate its shape begins with the teacher the first moment the student walks into the classroom. What the teacher models, exudes, and demonstrates is what the student will internalize in shaping a conception of the teacher. Pugach (2006) puts it this way:

> As the teacher, you have the opportunity—and responsibility—to develop the tone of the classroom, the feeling students get when they enter, the sense they have that it is a place they want to be. Although the physical environment is not an unimportant issue, it is the tone you set as the teacher that has the greatest influence on the kind of classroom you will have. Your interactions with your students—and the quality of these interactions under your guidance—tell them whether the classroom is a trustworthy environment for them. (371)

In order for teachers to examine their practice relative to building an environment of trust, it would be good to regularly and carefully consider the thought-provoking questions below (Pugach 2006, 368–371):

- Do I welcome my students in the classroom daily?
- Do I respect my students daily?
- Do I listen to my students? Do I encourage them to listen to each other?
- Do I sincerely want to know about my students' lives, their experiences, and what they value?
- Do I sensitively treat all my students fairly and justly?
- Do I extend a genuine level of respect to my students' families?
- Do I view myself as learner about my students' lives, or do they assume that the only learners in the classroom are themselves?

- What patterns might an outsider see if he or she observed the relationships I have established with my students and their families?
- Do I have trusting relationships with only some of my students or with all of them?
- Do I favor members of some racial and ethnic groups over others?
- What sources of feedback do I consider in gauging my success as a teacher who has developed a positive relationship with students?

OTHER SIDE OF THE SAME COIN

Respect is the other side of the same coin of trust. And because it is clearly implied that a trusting relationship functions in an environment that is illuminated by respect, it is worthy to spend a moment discussing the significance of its meaning.

Having its derivative in the Latin *respectus*, meaning to regard, to look back, to consider, the term "respect" is intertwined with the notions of judgment, evaluation, deliberation, acknowledgment, emotion, disposition, valuing, and motivation, to name a few. In short, respect is an aspect of life that daily arises in some fashion (Wawrytko 1982).[1]

For example, respecting the speed limit or the forest where wild animals roam is obviously different from respecting the office of a city, state, or national official and still different from granting respect to individuals. Even with the latter, the degree and type of respect given depends on multiple circumstances.

In the end, however, when dealing with human beings—whether it is in a family structure, in a classroom, at a community level, or a national/international level—respect (i.e., to regard or consider the other) is fundamental to the building of the human family.

Accordingly, in a classroom setting, a teacher establishes respect by first possessing a healthy respect for one's self, ability, and competence. In turn, a healthy self-respect ought to constructively radiate the following environment:

- A genuine respect for the other that places value on individual differences;
- Refraining from using sarcasm and derogatory vocabulary (e.g., "stupid," "loudmouth," "shut-up," and a host of other belittling remarks);
- Engaging in conversation with students that fosters encouragement, empathy, compassion, and an illumination of an overall support system;
- Welcoming the input of multiple points of view;
- Discerning the difference between thoughtful evaluation and self-righteous judgment; and
- Simply treating the other as each of us would like to be treated.

In short, as Deiro (1997) conveys, "students like teachers who think highly of them; students enjoy being around teachers who see them as bright and capable with bright futures in front of them" (198).

In closing, it is good to emphasize that a student–teacher relationship is obviously distinctly different from other types of relationships (e.g., parent/child, partner/partner, employer/employee). In other words, the diverse range of relationships we are all generally engaged in possesses certain accepted conventional values, mores, and boundaries. Moreover, within the multiple types of relationships that exist, there are certain said and unsaid power-related aspects that often play into the unfolding dynamics of the relationship, dictated by individual, family, cultural, religious, institutional, and organizational norms.

For example, in the student–teacher relationship, while it is fundamental that a flow of integrity must dictate the direction of the relationship, teachers need to not only be aware of the influential power they have, but also realize the necessary boundaries that ought to dictate that relationship. That is, first and foremost, the teacher is there to promote the cognitive, emotional, and intellectual growth and overall well-being of the student, which is bound in a relationship pattern that is obviously different from those that are personal in nature. In other words, to once again turn to the work of Pugach (2006):

> Teachers need to create the conditions in which their students will be motivated to learn . . . Being a teacher who creates a healthy classroom environment should not be confused with being a teacher who is "friends" with his or her students. The teacher's job is to teach students and make sure they learn. But teachers do not teach only content; they teach content to real, live students who deserve their respect and consideration. Moreover, students deserve teachers who are interested in them as individuals and as members of a particular racial or ethnic group. (368–371)

Teachers also engage in relationships with others who also "deserve their respect and consideration," leading into the next chapter, in which those other relationship patterns will be explored.

NOTE

1. http://plato.stanford.edu/entries/respect/.

TEN

Other Relationships

Parents/Caregivers, Colleagues, and the Wider Community

> *Efforts at education reform and other measures aiming to raise achievement levels will be more successful if schools first establish trust-based relationships with parents and their communities.*
>
> (Khalifa, Arnold, and Newcomb 2015, 21)

When a baby enters the world, s/he is at the mercy of those who will feed, bathe, and take care of her/his every need. And one of those critical needs is for the growing infant to feel a sense of security, which aids in healthy development and spurs on exploring her/his new surroundings. To put another way, through parental–child interactions that are caring, appropriate, predictable, and consistent, the infant develops a healthy sense of attachment (Siegel and Hartzell 2003).

This dynamic cultivates a state of being that is secure, enabling the likelihood of cognitive, social, and emotional development that is balanced and connected (Siegel and Hartzell 2003). As the child begins school, and the more parents are involved in the child's schooling life, the more likelihood the young person will academically succeed (Ryan and Cooper 2013). The latter narrative is the ideal that all children hope to experience in their formative years, providing a firm foundation in enriching the developmental growth process.

Not all children, however, are born into settings that are ideal when it comes to parental interaction and involvement. The absence or an inconsistent lack of parental/caregiver presence and participation can negatively affect a growing infant with respect to his/her attitude, level of security, confidence, self-concept, and school-readiness level.

In short, parents/caregivers of students naturally come from diverse backgrounds with respect to how they have or have not bonded with their children, certainly having implications for the classroom teacher. Yet whatever those differences may be, the quality of relationships parents have formed with their own children, the dispositions their children bring to the school setting, and the school readiness level they possess, the task of the teacher is to work toward establishing a coexisting relationship with all parents.

To reiterate, success in school is likely to occur when a child is wrapped in a secure family structure that fosters a healthy sense of attachment, coupled with parental involvement in the child's education. The assumption is that the teacher also realizes the importance of continuing a relational pattern that is secure, competent, and appropriate with both the child and parent.

But what about the child who, for a variety of reasons, comes from an insecure home environment with an unhealthy sense of attachment, where s/he may be food deprived, and where the parent/caregiver appears to be absent or uninvolved, resulting in the child possibly lacking in the social, cognitive, and emotional skills once s/he enters the classroom door?

It is in this place that teachers can be enormously challenged, but it is also in this place where they can see opportunity in heightening their awareness level, realizing all the more why cultivating a relationship with the child is extraordinarily important.

While the child may enter the classroom door seemingly already "wired" in how s/he acts, and what s/he does and does not do, especially in displays of emotional inappropriateness and lack of school readiness and preparation, this dispositional place can be "rewired" in how the teacher lovingly and patiently relates to the child. In other words:

> It's never too late to create positive change in a child's life . . . A nurturing relationship with someone other than with a parent in which the child feels understood and safe provides an important source of resilience, a seed in the child's mind that can be developed later on as the child grows. Relationships with relatives, teachers, childcare providers, and counselors can provide an important source of connection for the growing child. These relationships don't replace a secure attachment with a primary caregiver, but they are a source of strength for the child's development. (Siegel and Hartzell 2003, 102–3)

In the end, whether it is the nurturing of relationships with students, parents/caregivers, and colleagues (to be discussed below), it is ultimately a necessary act of the will for teachers to engage in this important bonding for the positive impact it can have on the teaching and learning process (Hargreaves 2001).

In that light, therefore, when it comes to establishing collaborative coexisting relationships with parents/caregivers, the following are some suggestions:

- Through your own competence, confidence, and communication skills, convey to parents/caregivers that their child is in good hands.
- Initiate and build an environment of dialogue, trust, and respect.
- Extend an enthusiastic hand of welcome and consistently maintain that openness.
- Personalize interactions and be aware of the way you speak, the vocabulary that is used, the tone that is emanated, and the body language that radiates.
- Let parents/caregivers know who you are, why you are a teacher, and what your philosophy of education is.
- Let parents/caregivers know that their input is sincerely welcomed and necessary (presumably, they know their child best).
- Realize that, as a teacher, you are also a learner.
- Let parents/caregivers know what a typical day looks like for their child.
- Refrain from judging parents/caregivers in the way they dress, speak, write, and from what economic class they are from.
- Be culturally responsive, and realize the strength in diversity.
- Stay in regular communication with parents through hand written notes, weekly agendas, phone calls, email, and so on.
- Realize that some parents/caregivers may be intimidated because of language barriers, education level, or injurious schooling experiences. In other words, reach out.
- Don't assume that silence/lack of follow up from parents/caregivers is "not caring."
- Be sensitive to parents'/caregivers' work schedule, struggles, and challenges.
- Sensitively work toward disarming obstacles of all types by taking initiative to convey genuine interest.
- Stay away from gossip of all sorts.
- Realize that parents/caregivers and other family members are your greatest source of information.

RELATIONSHIPS WITH COLLEAGUES

Particularly in school systems that are hierarchal in nature, there are obvious certain power structures at play in the relationship patterns that exist (e.g., teacher–principal–superintendent). Principals and others in leadership positions have an ethical responsibility to be aware of their leadership styles, the way they interact with others, and whether they are acutely aware of fostering a collegial environment. While beyond the scope of purpose here in exploring effective leadership styles of school administrators, one style, however, that thoughtfully is conducive toward fostering a collegial environment is a transformational leadership approach.

This approach is one that functions via a collaborative effort *through* people as opposed to *over* people, fostering professionalism, the sharing of decisions, and teacher empowerment. In other words, where teachers are genuinely valued, are engaged in a supportive collegial environment, and where trust is realized, the impact is not only positively manifested in the way teachers approach their craft, but also plays a significant role in shaping the quality of their commitment and longevity in the teaching profession (Eginli 2007; Leithwood and Poplin 1992).

To be sure, no different than any other human relationship patterns, the building of collegial relationships requires effort in building a supportive atmosphere of trust, cooperation, and collaboration. In short, the depth of the quality of the relationships among the adult population working in the school has a significant impact on student success, accomplishment, and innovation (Barth 2006; Fullan 2001).

RELATIONSHIP WITH THE WIDER COMMUNITY

Teachers are important public figures in the community; in fact, they are the ultimate public figures in their pivotal role of moving a community forward. While teachers are obviously entitled to private lives, the reality, however, once they step out in the community—no matter how far and how wide it is from their local school community—they not only represent individual selves, but also because of the uniqueness of their work and the important relational aspect of it, the title of "teacher" is not removed.

In other words, similar to those in the ministry, the essence of representing "teacher" is necessarily linked to a character that exudes a certain ethical, moral, and honorable way of being. And the authenticity of that ethical character is necessarily determined by the synchronization of both a private and public way of being (refer also back to chapter 3). Campbell (2003) explains an aspect of this moral agency in this way:

> The ethical teacher is, by necessity, an ethical person. One who only lies and cheats for personal gain or who is callous towards the feelings of others is unlikely to transform into a principled person of integrity upon becoming a teacher. And, the teacher who strives to empathize with students and colleagues, who aims to be fair, careful, trustworthy, responsible, honest, and courageous in the professional role probably understands and appreciates the importance of such virtues in everyday life as well. The moral and ethical principles that teachers them-

selves uphold in the ways they interact with students and others and in their approach to their professional responsibilities provide the basis of one aspect of their moral agency. (23)

Indeed, because teachers are public figures, what they say, how and what they communicate, and how they act, the public is watching.[1]

Again, this does not mean that teachers are not permitted to have a good time, to "let their hair down," and simply be comfortably disarmed in what they do outside of school. It does mean, however, that teachers need to be wise and discerning as to what they say and do in public (including social media use). For example, a group of teachers at a restaurant speaking loudly confidential information about their students would be woefully inappropriate, or gossiping about other teachers would simply be out of bounds. In other words, as Manvell (2009) asserts, "teaching is a highly visible profession. You are in the public eye and always on duty as a representative of your school and the teaching profession . . . If you can't justify it, don't say, write, or do it! . . . Write, speak, and act like you are educated, wise, have integrity, and are thoughtful. Model what you expect" (133).

In closing, whether teachers are going to the store, attending civic events, or participating in any number of activities, they are in relationships with the wider community. This position of being called "teacher" is an earned privilege that necessarily must function with a sense of making wise choices, monitoring what is shared, and handling with care the influencing power a teacher possesses.

NOTE

1. This is along the same stream of thinking as in the book *The Students Are Watching* by Sizer and Sizer (1999), where the authors gently remind teachers that students are continuously watching, taking in, and absorbing behaviors teachers model, the values they exude, the work ethic they illuminate, and the degree of trust and respect they give, all which shapes their opinion of what kind of teachers and people they are. As Sizer and Sizer put it, *"they watch us all the time* . . . The students, that is . . . They learn from all the watching and listening . . . We teachers and other adults who care about children should attend to even the humblest of these actions [what we say and do] and these dangers, so that we may teach our students—and ourselves—a worthy way of life" (xvii–xviii, author's emphasis).

ELEVEN

To Be in Relationships Is to Celebrate Diversity

> *Multicultural education is consequently as important for middle-class White suburban students as it is for students of color who live in the inner city. Multicultural education fosters the public good and the overarching goals of the commonwealth.*
>
> (Banks 2014, xiii)

As was suggested in chapter 6, we are "hardwired" to be in relationships, and as was pointed out in chapter 7, students arrive through the classroom door just as they are, representing a variety of cultural influences, races, ethnicities, languages, economic classes, and family structures. The question for classroom teachers is, therefore, are they aware of those diverse differences, and do they see strength in fostering a schooling environment that is mindfully multicultural in its approach? To more concretely explain, consider the following scenario.

Picture a group of three hundred teachers being required to attend a professional-development workshop on the theme of diversity. The obvious assumption driving the purpose of the workshop is that concepts, practices, and attitudes regarding diversity are important considerations for educators to reflectively ponder and discuss as it relates to their work. As all the teachers settle in their seats, the speaker begins the workshop by asking a nonintimidating question: "With a show of raising your hands, is diversity sensitivity important?"

All three hundred teachers lackadaisically, but spontaneously, raise their hands and mutter a response in agreement. The reason for their lackluster reply is two-fold: first, the professional-development workshop was mandated and for multiple reasons teachers were resistant to being there; and second, all the attending teachers knew what the "right answer" was to the unremarkable question.

The idea that all the teachers raised their hand in the affirmative on the issue of whether diversity is important may seemingly be an innocuous observable matter. But it is not. On the one hand, it is, of course, good that all the teachers positively affirmed the importance of diversity sensitivity; on the other hand, do, in fact, all the teachers authentically believe, think, and live that response in their practice? Perhaps yes; perhaps no. And particularly for those in the latter category, they nevertheless raised their hand in agreement because they knew that was the right thing to do in a public space, in front of their peers, whether they believed in their response or not.

Teachers are obviously a microcosm of the diverse society in which we live. And with respect to sensitivities and awareness related to race, ethnicity, gender, language, and other ways that comprise our pluralistic society at large, some of us proudly embrace diversity, others are lukewarm, still others naïve, and then there are those who in various degrees are racist, bigoted, biased, and intolerant in thought and action.

Teachers are a subset of society, and while we would like to think that they all genuinely embrace the notion of diversity, the reality is that not all of them do. Yet, teachers are smart enough to know what the "right answer" is to the speaker's question. And this is a critical point. Children who come from diverse backgrounds sitting before a teacher do not care to have a teacher who knows what the "right answer" is regarding the diversity that the teacher faces; rather, children desire a teacher who believes in them *because* of their diversity.

A QUESTION OF THE HEART, MIND, AND ATTITUDE

Embracing the celebration of diversity is a question of the heart, a question of disposition, a question of attitude, and a question of a habit of mind, concepts that were discussed in section I. To reiterate, Dewey (1933) reminds educators that for one to grow in thought and awareness, it is imperative to critically examine one's beliefs, values, and ways of doing, which must then be filtered through an attitudinal process that includes open-mindedness, whole-heartedness, and being mindfully responsible.

Indeed, the implication of such a process, if it is to be genuinely embraced, can be simultaneously invigorating, affirming, and challenging. Again, we ultimately teach who we are. And who we are when it comes to our viewpoints and concepts regarding diversity is one of the most important tasks a teacher must critically self-examine.

This self-examination includes the realization that with respect to P–12 schools, students of color comprise over 40 percent of the population, and by 2020 that number is estimated to rise to 50 percent. And in many states, African Americans, Latinos, Asian Americans, and Native American are the majority population in public schools (Gollnick and Chinn 2013). Moreover, this self-examination naturally also includes the exploration of a contextual grasp of the historical circumstances that have led to a concept penned as multicultural education (see Gollnick and Chinn 2013; Delpit 2012; Bennett 2007; Banks 2006; Pai and Adler 2001; Freire 1990, 1985).

In other words, this contextualization possesses a basic conception that as a result of when the Europeans first touched the shores of the Americas in 1492 and the reverberating effects of the Transatlantic Slave Trade, the ground was laid for the later need of an education that is multicultural (among others, see the work of Eltis and Richardson 2010; Davis 2010; Blight 2010; Loewen 2010, 2007; Gutiérrez 1993.) To put it another way, in order to understand the present, we must understand the past; in order to not repeat the past, we must not forget the past; and in order to move forward we must, on the one hand, be mindful of the progress that has been made, and on the other hand, remain actively attentive and involved where change is still needed.

Indeed, multicultural education is ultimately a response to a one-world point of view, namely Eurocentric. This, therefore, can be a self-examination riddled with intimidation, particularly for a teaching population that is 83 percent European American and mostly female, many of whom have historically "been taught to view events, situations, and our national history primarily from the perspectives of mainstream historians and social scientists sympathetic to the dominant groups within our society" (Banks 2006, 331).[1]

In fact, Gay (2005) argues that many teachers are not only reluctant to embrace the idea of multicultural education, but flat out resist it. This resistance is due to a number of factors, such as lack of knowledge, contextual pedagogical understandings, lived experiences with minority groups, the overwhelming nature of the topic, and discomfort, leading many teachers "to avoid dealing with these difficult issues among themselves, as well as with their students" (xviii).

But avoidance cannot be an option, nor silence, nor an acquiescence to the status quo, nor an acceptance of the alternative to multicultural education, which is an education that is monocultural (Cummins 2008). That is, a "monocultural education is written in the 'certainties' of the Crusades and the Inquisition; the smug brutalities of slavery; the casual eradication of language, culture, and identity in boarding schools inflicted on Native American children; and the contemporary claims of fundamentalist groups, from various religious persuasions, to have exclusive access to ultimate truths" (Cummins 2008, xvi).

There is a plethora of guiding, helpful literature that is available for the classroom teacher in order to better understand, make sense of, and sensitively address concepts and issues related to multicultural education, providing informative definitions of terms and concepts, how and what to teach relative to multicultural education, do's and don'ts, and so on. The point here is not so much in that vein, leaving that to the notable work of many others. Rather, the objective here is to foster awareness, one which can lead to further readings (see Gollnick and Chinn 2013; Delpit 2012; Bennett 2007; Banks 2006; Pai and Adler 2001; Freire 1990, 1985).

The assumption is that awareness leads to revelation, which leads to deeper examination, which leads to action, leading to change. This is not some dreamy utopian ideal, but a belief in the conscientious effort of the teacher who desires to grow in knowledge in order to better contextualize his/her practice, despite what may be an overwhelming, challenging, and even uncomfortable theme. In short, for the classroom teacher, multicultural education is not a formulistic affair; rather, it is an affair of awareness, an affair of nurturing one's epistemological curiosities in order to be fair and just when working with a diverse student population.

MULTIPLE PERSPECTIVES OF MULTICULTURAL EDUCATION

The contemporary unfolding of multicultural education has been a fifty-year affair, with the injection of multiple perspectives and approaches in the schools. Rooted in themes related to a pluralistic outlook, there are multiple, interrelated ways to describe multicultural education. The following are but a few perspectives:

> An important goal of multicultural education is to improve race relations and to help all students acquire the knowledge, attitudes, and skills needed to participate in cross-cultural interactions and in personal, social, and civic action that will help make our nation more democratic and just. Multicultural education is consequently as important for middle-class White suburban students as it is for students of color who live in the inner city. Multicultural education fosters the public good and the overarching goals of the commonwealth. (J. A. Banks 2010, x)

> The specific aims of multicultural education . . . are (1) the cultivation of an attitude of respect for and appreciation of the worth of cultural diversity, (2) the promotion of the belief in the intrinsic worth of each person and an abiding interest in the well-being of the larger society, (3) the development of multicultural competencies to function effectively in culturally varied settings, and (4) the facilitation of educational equity for all regardless of ethnicity, race, gender, age, or other exceptionalities. Developing an appreciation of cultural diversity as enriching rather than harmful to individuals or the national unity is the first aim of multicultural education. (Pai and Adler 2001, 112)

> Multicultural education in the United States is an approach to teaching and learning that is based on democratic values and beliefs and affirms cultural pluralism within culturally diverse societies in an interdependent world . . . Multicultural education consists of four interactive dimensions: the movement toward equity, or equity pedagogy; curriculum reform, or rethinking the curriculum through multiple perspectives; multicultural competence, the process of becoming conscious of your own as well as other cultural perspectives as a foundation for informed cross-cultural interactions; and teaching toward social justice, the commitment to combat prejudice and discrimination of all kinds, especially racism, sexism and classism. (Bennett 2007, 4)
>
> Essentially, **multicultural education** can be defined as a process of educational reform that assures that students from all groups (racial, ethnic, socioeconomic, ability, gender, etc.) experience educational equality, success, and social mobility. (Cushner, McClelland, and Safford 2012, 22)

While the above is a small sampling of the meaning and purpose of multicultural education, the various descriptions do, however, collectively capture what all the literature generally says about it, resulting in the emergence of common multicultural education themes.

That is, multicultural education is about respect, dignity, equality, justice, opportunity, freedom, hope, love, and unity. With ups, downs, successes, and failures, the historical road to fostering a system that believes in the hope of multiculturalism and the realization of what it means to celebrate diversity begins with entering into relationships with a diverse student population.

NOTE

1. Eighty-five percent of the teachers in elementary schools are female, and 58 percent are female at the high-school level (Gollnick and Chinn 2013).

Section III

The Goal Is to Inspire (An Artistic Endeavor)

Teachers who function artistically in the classroom not only provide children with important sources of artistic experience, they also provide a climate that welcomes exploration and risk-taking and cultivates the disposition to play.

(Eisner 2002, 162)

TWELVE
The Character of Inspiration

Inspiration involves being filled and being moved. Inspiration provides psychological and spiritual sustenance and often provides an education in values reminding us of what is most important.

(Hart 2000, 50)

The idea of being inspired possesses a discernible personal connective dimension. Consider the writer and his thought; the poet and her prose; the painter and his easel; the musician and her instrument; the scientist and an experimental flask; the mystic and the otherworldly; and the mentor and the mentee, to name a few examples.

Whether one is writing a book, a poem, painting a picture, or mentoring another, there is something sustainably powerful that prompts the inspiration for one to faithfully remain committed to the encounter. Indeed, the flowering of inspiration is a result of some kind of connection with people, experiences, and multiple other triggering events (see appendix A for a historical context of inspiration as a concept).

While inspiration is an abstract concept and it can be challenging to explain "what it looks like" or what its characteristics are, Thrash and Elliot (2004, 2003) are helpful in providing a synthesized concrete picture for us with their tripartite conceptualization of it. First, there is a natural transcendent aspect to it, meaning that inspiration captivatingly leads one toward something better, more important, or greater than oneself, enabling a view of possibilities that otherwise are not seen through our typical daily lives; second, inspiration is a result of evocation, implying that it is unwilled or induced by something outside of one's control; and third, inspiration triggers motivation, providing an energized aura in moving one to act.

Adding to that picture of what inspiration looks like, Hart (2000, 1998) further makes the interrelated point that inspiration, couched in trust, appreciation, acceptance, and love, alters one's boundaries, which moves one to a greater connectedness to self, to the other, or the object of concentration (i.e., a writer to his words; a songwriter to her lyrics, etc.). In addition, inspiration fosters an openness that otherwise is not there, allowing for a receptivity and availability to be filled with a new awareness or illumination.

Thus, with that sense of connectedness, openness, and clarity, inspiration cultivates a feeling of vibrancy or vitality, exhibited in excitement and enthusiasm toward action. Finally, and perhaps most importantly, the idea of being inspired is not a phenomenon that is reserved for a select few, but rather it is an event in which all are participants, playing a pivotal role in our ways of knowing, understanding, and being.

TEACHER AS MENTOR: INSPIRATIONAL EFFORTS

With a natural personal connective dimension to its unfolding, the vibrancy of inspiration clearly has implications for the classroom teacher. Teachers are indeed in that unique privileged position to stimulate students in such a way to impact the way they think, what they think, the decisions they make, and the actions they take. To state another way, the fragrance vitalizing the air of inspiration is a provocative concept that ultimately leads to movement.

For example, Anne Sullivan, Jaime Escalante, Erin Gruwell, and Herman Boone are four notable educators who have been recognized for their inspirational mentoring efforts. As Hart (2000) puts it, "inspiration is consuming and contagious, cultivated by our mere association with something or someone" (45). In that light, Sullivan, Escalante, Gruwell, and Boone, a diverse group of educators, are briefly discussed, underscoring the resolve that steered the nature of their inspirational mentoring efforts.

ANNE SULLIVAN

Anne Sullivan (1866–1936) was an extraordinary teacher who is especially known for her ingenious approach to teaching Helen Keller. However, the likelihood of Sullivan even becoming a teacher, much less an exceptional one, is a remarkable narrative in and of itself. Born in Massachusetts, Sullivan grew up in poverty, and at a very young age she was inflicted with trachoma, an eye disease that greatly incapacitated her sight. Her mother died when she was eight years old, and she was abandoned by her abusive father, who sent her to live in a notorious group home called Tewksbury Almshouse. Sullivan's strong character, however, kept her afloat with the idea that getting a good education was vital in helping her to rise above her circumstances (Nielsen 2010; Eldred 1997).

Through her determination and surgery that somewhat helped her eyesight, Sullivan excelled at the Perkins School of the Blind, leading her to be selected as valedictorian for her class. Upon graduation, Sullivan was later recommended to be the governess for Helen Keller in Tuscumbia, Alabama. Naturally incorporating the sense of touch, it was through an ingenious teaching and learning approach, one that connected words with objects, that Sullivan brought light to Keller's world of darkness and voice to one who was once thought mute. Though working with Helen Keller was an extraordinary challenge, Sullivan was clearly driven by an unwavering commitment to her, prompting worldwide attention for her creative initiatives and inspirational efforts (Nielsen 2010; Eldred 1997).

JAIME ESCALANTE

Jaime Escalante (1930–2010) is remembered for his untiring efforts in his work with struggling high-school students at Garfield High School in East Los Angeles, California, where drug use and violence were commonplace. Born and raised in Bolivia, Escalante, with extremely limited English skills, moved to California in his early thirties because of political turmoil and in search of a better life for his family. Even though he was a popular mathematics teacher for several years in his home country, Escalante was not certified to teach in the United States. He therefore worked a variety of jobs, spending much time learning English, eventually earning a degree and certification to teach high school, where he held high expectations for all his students, regardless of their life circumstances (Gilroy 2006; Mathews 1989).

As a teacher of advanced math and calculus and somewhat controversial in his instructional approach, working with mostly poor Latino students, many of his colleagues and community members blatantly let him know that his students were not capable of such an advanced curriculum. Escalante was not only disturbed by those attitudes, but also was at times confrontational with those who held them (Gilroy 2006; Mathews 1989).

Fueled by a genuine love and driven by what he called *ganas*, or the intense desire to motivate, Escalante recognized the potential in all his students. And despite seriously jeopardizing his health and making great family sacrifices, he worked with his students before and after school, and on weekends, too. When his students passed the advanced placement calculus exam, a charge was levied that his students cheated (Gilroy 2006).

Escalante was outraged, protested, and was adamant that racism is what directed the charge of cheating. Nevertheless, the students once again took the advanced exam and once again indisputably passed, all of which was the central theme of the book *Jaimie Escalante: The Best Teacher in America*, and the popular motion picture, *Stand and Deliver*, starring the Oscar-nominated actor Edward James Olmos (Gilroy 2006).

ERIN GRUWELL

Against the wishes of her father, who feared for her safety, Erin Gruwell (1969–) taught at Woodrow Wilson High School in Long Beach, California, where students were challenging and were at great risk of dropping out. When she first started working with her students, Gruwell learned quickly that they did not quite like her, were not fond of writing, and were exasperated with a scripted curriculum that was not relevant to their experiences. They called her names, made fun of her, and demonstrated very little respect (Freedom Writers and Gruwell 1999).

Undeterred and grounded in hope, Gruwell earnestly sought ways to make meaningful connections with her students, particularly through the medium of writing. Taking the creative initiative and purchasing alternative books with her own money, Gruwell sought stories, authors, and events that were meaningful to her students. They discussed the lyrics of Tupac and the prose of Alice Walker, Amy Tan, and Gary Soto; this captivated the interest of her audience, slowly breaking down their resistance. They visited the Museum of Tolerance in Los Angeles, where the students were profoundly impacted by the museum's emphasis on the Holocaust (Freedom Writers and Gruwell 1999).

The students also raised money to fly Miep Gies from Amsterdam to visit Woodrow Wilson High School. Gies is known for her heroic efforts to hide Anne Frank. Gruwell and her students also worked hard to have Zlata Filipovic come visit their school. From Sarajevo, Filipovic had her diaries published, which chronicled the atrocities of the war in her country. In particular, it was this latter experience that prompted Gruwell to have her students write their own stories, their own diaries. With unbridled motivation, the students were genuinely inspired and earnestly wrote; their work eventually turned into a best-selling book titled *The Freedom Writers Diary*, and a hit movie, *Freedom Writers* (Freedom Writers and Gruwell 1999).

HERMAN BOONE

In 1971, when the war in Vietnam was fueling the nation's collective consciousness and racial tensions continued to grip the country in turmoil, the city of Alexandria, Virginia, was in the midst of integrating their schools. It was during that time that Herman Boone (1935–), a teacher and a coach, was selected to coach the football team at T.C. Williams High School in Alexandria. Boone viewed coaching as an avenue to help shape attitudes and to positively impact the lives of young people (Collett, Kelly, and Sobolewski 2010).

The integration of T.C. Williams High School was hostilely riddled with tension and heightened even more because Boone, who is African American, was appointed as football coach over a popular white coach. To be sure, Boone faced much resistance from the community, but his commanding leadership fostered an environment that did not allow for prejudice to poison the attitude of the players and the coaches (Collett, Kelly, and Sobolewski 2010).

In his efforts to work with those young men, Boone brought them to Gettysburg College to hold a football camp. They also visited the grounds of the Battle of Gettysburg where Boone used that excursion as a teachable moment, explaining how terribly divided the country was because of race. This had a remarkable impression on the players. As the football camp unfolded, the players' awareness of the destructiveness of intolerance grew, moving them to think more about the purpose of team and working together (Collett, Kelly, and Sobolewski 2010).

In the end, Boone's energies in stressing equality, tolerance, and justice had a monumental impact on bringing the team together, culminating in a victory in the 1971 Virginia State High School Championship game. The influence of Boone's civil rights work is depicted in the popular motion picture *Remember the Titans*, starring Denzel Washington (Collett, Kelly, and Sobolewski 2010).

FOUR COMMON CHARACTERISTICS

In summary, the lives, vocations, circumstances, and challenges of each of the educators described above are obviously different. For all four of them, however, four distinct common characteristics emerge. First, each one is driven by a cause greater than him/herself. And that cause is the welfare, realization, and quality of life for their students. For Sullivan, the central focus was bringing light to Helen Keller's darkness; for Escalante, it was fostering belief in the potential of high-school students who were subjected to an environment of constant low expectations; for Gruwell, it was making meaningful connections with inner-city students who saw schooling as detestably irrelevant; and for Boone, it was teaching the importance of equality and justice for all in the midst of racial tension.

Second, in their unique ways, Sullivan, Escalante, Gruwell, and Boone demonstrate unique passion for what they do, meaning they are authentically driven, persistent, and compelled to qualitatively mentor. Third, each of them is rooted in hope, implying there is a light, a way, and an expectation for the bettering of the lives of their students. And, finally, each is heroically selfless, indicative of their sacrifice, belief, and connective possibilities in their role as educators.

Through their work, Sullivan, Escalante, Gruwell, and Boone are but four examples of countless known and unknown inspiring educators who stimulate and courageously facilitate movement and growth in the human family.

THIRTEEN

Inspiration and the Autobiographical Nature of Teaching

The mediocre teacher tells. The good teacher explains. The superior teacher demonstrates. The great teacher inspires.

(Ward 1968, 16)

The primary goal of one who teaches is to inspire, because inspiration deeply touches us and meaningfully moves us. And an educator who inspirationally teaches is one who has been inspired to teach with deep meaning, deliberate purpose, loving hope, and a focused vision. A beginning step toward realizing the role of inspiration, therefore, is to first be clear about the concept itself, and to be aware of what it is that personally inspires, moves, and roots oneself. Clearly, Anne Sullivan, Jaime Escalante, Erin Gruwell, and Herman Boone were rooted in something greater than themselves.

By its nature, inspiration is something that is fostered, not forced; it is welcomed, not coerced; it is invited, not imposed; it is authentic, not contrived; it offers a sense of joy and excitement, not monotony and boredom; it is viewed with awe, not compulsion; and it permeates in a spirit of wonder, not in an air of mandates. Inspiration is indeed decisively linked as an agency of influence. And a classroom that is pervaded with a climate of welcome, invitation, joy, excitement, awe, and wonder is an environment that cultivates an influential setting, which stimulates meaningful teaching and learning.

It is equally true, however, that classroom environments that reek of coercion, compulsion, mandates, monotony, boredom, and imposition are oppressive spaces that turn that proverbial light-bulb out. To be sure, purposeful teachers are those who constantly gauge what kind of classroom climate they are promoting. As Haim Ginott (1972) contends in his popular timeless declaration:

> I have come to a frightening conclusion. I am the decisive element in the classroom. It is my personal approach that creates the climate. It is my daily mood that makes the weather. As a teacher, I possess tremendous power to make a child's life miserable or joyous. I can be a tool of torture or an instrument of inspiration. I can humiliate or humor, hurt or heal. In all situations it is my response that decides whether crisis will be escalated or de-escalated and a child humanized or dehumanized.

In short, the more teachers understand the inspiration that drives them, the motives that move them, the intent that guides them, and the dispositions that root them, the better likelihood they realize what it means to make meaningful connections with their diverse student population.

AUTOBIOGRAPHICAL NATURE OF TEACHING

The above comprehensively points toward the idea that there is a natural autobiographical element to the pedagogical process, suggesting that intrinsic in teaching is one's story. To state another way, the more examined our story, our being, the more we understand why we do what we do, implying that our autobiography is intimately linked to the curriculum and the teaching and learning process.

In fact, it is fair to say that pedagogy (see chapter 18) and curriculum are different sides of the same coin. As a conceptual point of reference, the term "curriculum" is a verb derived from the Latin infinitive *currere*, which is an action, or a journey, to run the course (Pinar 1994; Pinar and Grumet 1976). The assumption is that the inner dynamics of a person are inherent, thus becoming intimately involved in the curriculum, facilitating direction. That is, the curriculum becomes an inward journey, a human question (Slattery 1995).

As teachers consider the significance of what grounds them, the autobiographical nature of curriculum and its link to pedagogy—all of which is woven through the cultivation of meaningful relationships with their students—the element of inspiration thus acts as the energy that generates movement. Inspiration triggers the epiphanic moment; turns bright the proverbial light bulb; and distinctly moves one from right where s/he is. In the end, therefore, setting favorable conditions is fundamental to fostering an inspiring classroom setting, signifying that inspiration is not something that can be willed, but rather it is something that is invited or wooed under conditions that recognize its value (Hart 1998).

INVITING FAVORABLE CONDITIONS

The human touch, the human bond, the humanity of our being, is the foundation that most importantly irrigates the favorable conditions to invite inspiration. As Robert Sullo (1999) declares in his book *The Inspiring Teacher*, "the most important element in becoming an inspiring teacher is the ability to develop positive relationships with others . . . Inspiration is nurtured in relationships . . . The most important variable in any human interaction is the relationship itself" (17–93).

Sullo goes on to suggest that a teacher who is enthusiastic, passionate, and energized is one who fosters inspiration, nurturing a joyful, purposeful, supportive, and inclusive classroom. He further underscores that inspiring teachers are those who interact with students with respect, not sarcasm, building a community of learners in which the emphasis is learning as opposed to achievement.

Sir Kenneth Robinson (n.d.), a powerful advocate in highlighting the importance of creativity, not only rightly argues that education is about entering into relationships, but the process ought to be personal for every student, whereby teachers are "mentors, coaches, motivators, and lifelong sources of inspiration to their students."

Robinson (2009a) further asserts that creative capacities are inherent within all human beings, and that our schools need to do a better job of cultivating a diverse and rich curriculum in order to better capture the diverse gifts, talents, and imaginations of all students. In other words, "it's a fundamental human truth that people perform better when they're in touch with things that inspire them. For some people, it's gymnastics; for some people, it's playing the blues; and for some people, it's doing calculus" (Robinson 2009b, 25). In short, diverse curricula that work to tap into inherent differences are curricula approaches that are more likely to cultivate an inspiring classroom climate that moves students to fall in love with learning.

Naturally aware that the idea of education is more than just what is confined in school, Howard Gardner (2000), the architect of what is known as "multiple intelligences"—while clear about the importance of the disciplines, standards, the expertise of the teacher, and the natural place of assessment—favors a system of education that is student-centered, which pays attention to individual differences and developmentally appropriate sensitivities. Moreover, Gardner argues for a schooling environment that is personalized, individualized, and one that promotes enjoyment in learning and cultivates a wide range of student interest.

Different than Gardner's point, but certainly with its parallels, Palmer (2007) argues that a good teacher is one who knows how to thread that balance between a student-centered and a subject-centered classroom environment. The latter, in its extreme, is devoid of a sense of student presence, and the former, in its extreme, can lead to greatly compromising the quality of the teaching and learning process.

According to Palmer, the variable that rightly bridges a student-centered and subject-centered gap is passion. In other words, a teacher who is passionate about the subject matter is one who enthusiastically illuminates that subject as the center of attention, igniting energy in critically bonding the student with the discipline.

In the final analysis, the idea of inviting favorable conditions to spark an inspirational classroom setting begins first by establishing meaningful relationships, to personalize an approach that works to make connections, and to realize that there is no one standard model or some kind of prescriptive formula, but to only be aware that the ultimate goal is to inspire. Perhaps Weeks-Channel (2010) puts it best: "As an educator, inspiring others to greatness is as vital as oxygen to life . . . Great teachers are intoxicated by the opportunities of inspiring to greatness" (1). And to inspirationally teach is to artistically teach, the theme of the following chapter.

FOURTEEN

Inspiration Leads to an Artistic Act

Yet in the end, the making of wine is an art.
(Eisner 1991, 65)

Defining what is considered art is an age-old debate, perhaps best exemplified when modern art (c. 1880s–1970s) or contemporary art (c. 1970s to present) emerged on the scene with their various expressions of their craft. Unlike the era where artists generally depicted scenes of reality or of a religious theme typically commissioned by patrons, modern art moved away from traditional approaches and explored subject matter dictated by individual artists, experimenting with color, technique, and theme.

For example, Pablo Picasso, with his introduction of cubism, was a clear distancing from the centuries-held Western tradition of art, say of Michelangelo and other Renaissance artists. And more different from Michelangelo and Picasso is the artist Jackson Pollock, who was Jungian influenced, abstractly depicting his work with social and psychological themes.

And still even more different from those three luminaries, there is a continuous flow of contemporary artists of various genres who have exhibited provocative, if not controversial, art forms, portrayed in paintings, architecture, poetry, music, and sculpture. These are but a few examples that illustrate that the expressive nature of art is an eclectic endeavor, often sparking heated debate over what is considered art and what is not.

Merriam-Webster (2012) defines art as something that is created with imagination and skill that is beautiful or that expresses important ideas or feelings. Because art involves creativity, originality, expression, and imagination, it is a qualitative affair navigating through the convergence of value, religious, and cultural systems, as well as a confluence of political persuasions, generational differences, individual tastes, collective tastes, and signs-of-the-times events and realities.

Ultimately, therefore, art is an affair of the aesthetic, conventionally associated with the various artistic activities discussed above. But, by definition, expressions of art are much more than that, meaning that it is also linked to such activities as dance, sport, oration, music, photography, and a host of other human endeavors, which naturally include the act of teaching. The intuitiveness of creativity, originality, expression, feeling, and imagination is indeed an integral part of teaching.

The implication, therefore, is:

> That teachers, like painters, composers, actresses, and dancers, make judgments based largely on qualities that unfold during the course of action. Qualitative forms of intelligence are used to elect, control, and organize classroom qualities, such as tempo, tone, climate, pace of discussion, and forward movement . . . The teacher's activity is not dominated by prescriptions or routines but is influenced by qualities and contingencies that are unpredicted. (Eisner 2002, 155)

And yet, while the latter is true, like the debate in the world of painting as to what is considered art, the notion of teaching as an art provokes the same type of debate. In other words, if teaching is an art, what does that artistic activity qualitatively look like? Before responding to that question, it is worthy to first explore the critical elements that inform the teacher in order to artistically teach.

TO BE A CONNOISSEUR

Elliot Eisner (1991) famously coined the concept "educational connoisseurship," suggesting that teaching is an art in recognizing, experiencing, and judging its qualitative nuances. In order to explain his point, Eisner reflects on what it takes to be a wine connoisseur, beginning with the basic premise that one first has access to the wine and has the ability to taste it. However, the tasting of it is inclusive of the idea that one perceptively experiences and takes in the quality of the taste and the aroma it sheds, in order to qualitatively compare the taste with that of other wines.

With respect to its appearance at the tipping of the glass and the "hang time" red wine exhibits, one considers the age and body of the wine. And whether it is red or white wine, there are different categories, classes, and qualities that comprise each brand, all slightly different in taste, texture, and aroma. To be able to qualitatively determine the multiple differences, one has to experience the wine over a long period of time in order to become a connoisseur, turning that endeavor into an art form.

Eisner (1991) explains it this way:

> Enologists [those who study wine] now are highly trained in the chemistry and science of making wine, yet in the end, the making of wine is an art. It is an art because the quality of wine depends on someone's being able to (1) experience the qualitative nuances of wine and (2) make judgments about the virtue of the qualities experienced. Even a recipe or a formula has its ultimate test in the qualities experienced when the wine is tasted. In the end, a qualitative experience is the 'measure' of wine quality, and not the formula. (65)

There are indeed numerous excellent classes and brands of wine, and it takes a connoisseur to "measure" the quality of each of them. This takes time and what Eisner (1991) calls "perceptivity" in order to keenly experience the relationships and differences among the various wines. In short, connoisseurs are those who come to know (Eisner n.d.).

The analogy is clear when it comes to the overwhelming qualitative nature of education. That is, for the educator, the movement toward connoisseurship is an epistemic journey of one who is conscious of the various relationships that intertwine the qualitative nature of education. In other words, "connoisseurship depends on high levels of qualitative intelligence in the domain in which it operates . . . Connoisseurship is the means through which we come to know the complexities, nuances, and subtleties of aspects of the world in which we have a special interest" (Eisner 1991, 64–68).

With differences exhibited in race, ethnicity, culture, gender, school readiness, learning style, attention span, curiosities, interests, personalities, and a host of other anticipated and unanticipated differences that enter the classroom door, there a teacher stands. The presumption is that the teacher holds a commanding grasp of her craft in order to work with those differences.

In other words, to paraphrase Eisner, the act of teaching is art because the quality of the way one teaches is informed by how one creatively weaves the craft in such a way that realizes the qualitative nuances involved in the process. Indeed, "classrooms are probably one of the most complex subjects of connoisseurship" (Eisner 1991, 66). To put it another way, the "formula" that puts in place the teaching act is not what gets it done; rather, the recognition of the qualitative nature of teaching with what Eisner calls an "enlightened eye" that can see beyond the formula is what gets it done.

Teaching is not an act that can be dualistically explained as either a science or an art, or even a part of both. Rather, teaching is an art that is informed by various social, psychological, and cognitive sciences. And as critical as those sciences are, they are only as good as the one who interprets, uses, or incorporates them into one's way of doing things.

Clearly, Jackson Pollock possessed a grasp of the craft of painting, Mikhail Baryshnikov the craft of ballet, and Martin Luther King Jr. the craft of oration. But it wasn't their manual understanding of the craft that grabbed our attention; rather, it was their ability to use their craft in such a way that art was witnessed. In other words, the expression of their art form enabled a profound relationship with their audience. Yet to try to explain in words the profoundness of that expression is near impossible. Artistry in teaching is like that. As Banner and Cannon (1997) assert, "we think we know great teaching when we encounter it, yet we find it impossible to say precisely what has gone into making it great" (3).

To be sure, the nuances involved in teaching such as the way we speak, how we speak, when we speak, what we speak, the body language involved in that speaking, and one's overall communication patterns are all qualitative endeavors in which teachers aim to make connections with their diverse student population (Flinders 1989). Moreover, these endeavors are flavored with—among other qualitative components—flexibility, compassion, patience, tolerance, appreciation, love, hope, kindness, firmness, understanding, and fairness.

Truly, the art of teaching cannot be precisely explained as to what it looks like, simply because teaching is an affair of the heart. An affair of the heart is ignited by inspiration. Inspiration works to connect. To make connections is to know. And to know is to be a connoisseur.

Section IV

The Glue That Is Educational Psychology

That psychology ought to help the educator, there can be no disagreement. In the first place the study of psychology has a high disciplinary value for the teacher. It develops the power of connected thinking and trains to logical habits of mind.

(Dewey 1964a, 196)

FIFTEEN
The Critical Relevance of Theory

Educational psychology cannot tell teachers what to do, but it can give them the principles to use in making a good decision.

(Slavin 2000, 3)

David Elkind (2000), a prominent psychologist and educator, passionately argues that teacher candidates ought to have child development as their major in order to become a child-development specialist, making the point that education is not about curriculum, assessment or methods, but rather about children and youth, which suggests that teachers who have "a strong foundation in child development can integrate what they learn about curriculum, assessment and management with what they know about how children of various ages think and learn" (111). To state another way, the strength of a teacher's knowledge base[1]—in thought and action—is critically determined relative to one's informed grasp of educational psychology, which unfolds through the craft of teaching.

Deriving from Latin, the word "psychology" is the study of the soul, later evolving to mean the study of the mind and human behavior. Drawing from a variety of cognitive and behavioral theorists, educational psychology, therefore, is a field of study on how we learn, how we teach, and the number of considerations that influence that process (Eggen and Kauchak 2004).

As Parankimalil (2012) contends, educational psychology is a science that, in scope of study, views the learner as the central theme of study with respect to the learning experience, the learning process, the learning environment, and the teacher, all of which is linked to concepts related to human behavior, growth and development, heredity, environment, personality, differences, and intelligence.

And while educational psychology casts from a wide net of thought, it is particularly informed by developmental theories; however, before engaging in a narrative of those critical theoretical constructs (see chapter 16), it is worthwhile to first underscore the importance of theory.

CRITICAL RELEVANCE OF THEORY

It is not uncommon for some to tune out when the term "theory" is encountered, citing it is "only" theory, and its relevance in practice is summarily dismissed.[2] To be sure, in the everydayness of teaching, teachers operate in the concrete, in the moment; and yet, whether they are aware of the theory that guides their approach and interaction or not, assuredly, some theoretical paradigm is guiding their practice.

For example, consider the notion of culturally responsive teaching and its relationship to behavior/classroom management. A teacher may genuinely respect cultural differences that comprise the classroom demographics, but in some areas may be lacking in her/his understanding of those differences as they relate to classroom management. To illustrate the point, let's say the teacher—as a young child—was raised to "look the person in the eye" when being disciplined by an authority figure (parent, teacher, etc.), and thus expects students to look at her/him whenever s/he delivers any behavior management measures.

The theory, therefore, that guides this teacher's thinking—whether s/he consciously realizes it or not—is that looking the authority figure in the eye is a sign of respect, something the teacher has incorporated in her/his practice as a universal truth while teaching a diverse student population.

Perhaps this approach may be culturally responsive and reasonable for some of his/her students. But this uninformed point of view is a problem for the children of any number of Native American tribes who may be in the class, for a sign of respect for them is *not* giving eye contact—but rather of bent head, looking downward—when being admonished by an elder standing in front of her/him. Being unaware of this cultural difference can clearly cause a misunderstanding in this teacher's class, simply based on the teacher's theory of doing things. In short, for a particular case such as this scenario, "what may have been culturally responsive in one place at one time may not be in another" (Khalifa, Arnold, and Newcomb 2015, 21).

In the above illustration, while the teacher may be sincere in her/his efforts, s/he would be sincerely wrong when working with Native American children when it comes to classroom management. Indeed, acting on uninformed or unaware theories can be a hit-or-miss proposition during the course of the nearly one thousand decisions a teacher makes daily. The implication here, of course, is that the more teachers are aware of the theory that drives their thinking, the more they are likely to consider the repercussions that go into the daily decisions they make relative to curriculum, teaching approach, and behavior management.

Slavin (2000) asserts that an important mark of a professional is that within the process of making informed decisions that impact his/her work, the educator is able to identify problems or concerns, considers the variety of perspectives in any given situation, draws on critical professional knowledge, is discerning on appropriate action, and is perceptive in judging consequences. And a significant part of that entire process is the awareness of the theoretical perspectives that drive the educator's decision-making process.

Succinctly providing a useful definition of theory, emphasizing that theories provide for a teacher an important guide, Eggen and Kauchak (2004) explain that "A theory is *a set of related principles derived from observations that, in turn, are used to explain additional observations*" (19, author's emphasis). Eisner (2002) further makes the point that while knowledge of theories is not to serve as a prescription, theories can be used as suggestive tools in providing the educator a focus in which the world can be understood. Continuing to explain, Eisner asserts:

> Theoretical frameworks, scientific or otherwise, are frames of reference that perform two extremely important functions. First, they serve as a means for identifying aspects of the reality to which they address themselves. Theories remind us of what to attend to by calling our attention to the theory's subject matter. For example, theories in sociology make vivid the social structure of the classroom, they illuminate class differences among pupils, and they describe friendship patterns and formal and informal sanctions. Psychological theory (depending on the specific theory being used) might address itself to questions of self-esteem or forms of reinforcement or the need to provide students with opportunities to practice the behavior they are expected to learn. What theories do in this regard is to help us focus attention on aspects of classroom life that we might otherwise neglect . . . Although no single theory in any of the social sciences is likely to be adequate to deal with the particular reality with which an individual teacher must cope, theories do provide generalizations that can be considered in one's reflective moments as a teacher. (156–57)

Again, in the aforementioned scenario, the teacher's particular approach to behavior management was misguided; however, had s/he been more aware of the assumptions and theories that inform culturally responsive teaching, s/he would have been better equipped in working with a diverse student population. This is simply but one concrete example that demonstrates the relevance of theory in the everydayness of teaching. As we move forward to the next chapter, pertinent theories that fall under the large umbrella of theories of development will be explored.

NOTES

1. To be discussed in Section V, teacher knowledge referred here is comprised of five interrelated components: knowledge of students, knowledge of subject matter, knowledge of pedagogy, knowledge of learning, and knowledge of classroom management.

2. Consider the book titled *No More Theories Please! A Guide for Elementary Teachers* (2009) by L. K. Masao. As the title of the book suggests, the author seems to downplay the relevance of theories, and argues that the principal premise that drives her text is rooted in the idea that "The procedures and plans discussed are not theories but, rather, the successful results of what has been implemented and proven to work in my classroom" (x). The author then proceeds to discuss in her text various ways classrooms should be organized, provides suggestions to write lesson plans, underscores the significance of routines, highlights ways to incorporate classroom behavior management, draws from Bloom's Taxonomy, and recognizes the importance of differentiated instruction. Yet, the irony is the author's thinking and the practical ideas presented are based on some type of theoretical framework. The point here is not so much a criticism of the book with respect to the practical ideas it shares, but it would have been good for the author to disclose that her ideas are rooted in theory. And, in fact, that theory is critical where educational practice is informed (Kirylo 2009).

SIXTEEN
Paving the Way Toward Child/ Developmental Psychology

John Locke and Jean-Jacques Rousseau

> *Childhood has its place in the scheme of human life. We must view the man as a man, and the child as a child . . . Treat your pupil according to his age . . . Each age and state of life has its own proper perfection, its own distinctive maturity.*
>
> (Rousseau 1762, 159–63)

Theories of human development guide the educator in understanding that from birth to adulthood, and even into the twilight years, the unfolding of life occurs through stages that Parkay and Hass (2000) identify as infancy, childhood, early adolescence, middle adolescence, late adolescence, and adulthood.

Notwithstanding individual differences and cultural influences, awareness of these stages helps explain how human beings physically, cognitively, and emotionally develop, and how we adapt, learn, and change. Indeed, for the educator, an understanding of human development emphasizes that working with children is a unique undertaking that does not view them as miniature adults, but as developing human beings who "think differently . . . see the world differently, and . . . live by different moral and ethical principles than adults do" (Slavin 2000, 28).

The latter assertion by Slavin has not always been the case; in fact, the early emergence of developmental theories largely came about as a response to the antiquated system that viewed children as miniature adults. This viewpoint was validated by the centuries-held preformationistic theories in which it was thought a tiny person was already preformed at the moment of conception, and simply continued to grow until delivery (Crain 2000).

During the medieval period, the notion that children were viewed as miniature adults was illustrated in artwork, such as depictions in paintings and sculptures whereby the characteristics of children, and even babies, were that of miniature adults. Moreover, during that era, by age 12, and sometimes even at a younger age, children were fully immersed in an adult world, with adult responsibilities, working as apprentices (e.g., farming, weaving, metal work, carpentry) and wearing adult-style clothing. And concepts related to speech, motor, and other child-developmental processes were largely ignored (Crain 2000). That is, there was an apparent lack of awareness that growing infants maturate in such a way that uniquely, individually, and developmentally defines them in the process of passing through childhood before entering into adulthood.

It was in the midst of the 1500s, with the introduction of the printing press, the spread of trade, the growth of cities, and new occupational opportunities such as law, banking, and government that the need for more schools and the emphasis on education became a high priority. Particularly for those in the middle class, this development had an impact on how children were viewed, what their roles ought to be, and what they should be responsible for. What rose to the top of the list for parents was that children receiving a formal education became a major priority, many desiring for their offspring to be in school well into the teenage years (Crain 2000).

This dramatic shift in thought and priority placed children in a new light, viewing them less as miniature adults, but rather as beings who were being shaped to grow into adulthood. Accordingly, this shift went against the grain, the feudal way of thinking and doing, rejecting "a society in which everyone's place was predetermined by birth. It sought a brighter future, pinning great hopes on education to bring it about. In so doing, it helped usher in the modern way of life" (Crain 2000, 4).

Yet while all of this was a move in the right direction on behalf of young people, they were still expected to dress as adults while attending school and were subjected to remaining in their seats for hours at a time. Moreover, the approach to schooling was majorly dictated by rote memorization, severe corporal punishment, and a lingering ignorance of the fact that children were different from adults in how they process, learn, and develop (Crain 2000).

As a clear response to this disturbing schooling approach, John Amos Comenius (1592–1670), a Czech education and religious leader, argued that children learn differently than adults do, implying that childhood is a unique stage of life in which learning occurs through experience. It was Comenius who published *Orbis Pictus* (*The World of Pictures*), a picture book for children, the first of its kind in Western education (Longstreet and Shane 1993).

Moreover, Comenius influenced John Locke and Jean-Jacques Rousseau, who are both recognized as pioneers in child psychology, launching the notion of environmentalism and learning theory (Locke), and the developmental tradition (Rousseau) (Crain 2000). The work of each will be discussed here, beginning with Locke.

JOHN LOCKE (1632–1704)

Born in England, Locke was a physician and philosopher who came to be known as a key originator of liberal philosophy, influencing the Enlightenment period with his conception of religious freedom and separation of church and state. In addition to his conception of the latter, his emphasis regarding human beings inherently possessing natural rights regarding life, liberty, and property greatly influenced the framers of the Declaration of Independence and the Constitution. And while Locke is momentously recognized as an influential voice in the shaping of the founding documents of the United States, he also significantly contributed to educational thought.

Most famously, Locke proposed that a newborn's mind is a "white paper, void of all characters, without any ideas" (Locke 1690). In other words, the infant's mind is a *tabula rasa* (blank slate), meaning that it is through experience with the outside environment that one comes to know. The idea that one learns or comes to know through experience is rooted in the idea of Francis Bacon's concept of empiricism.[1]

Contrary to Plato's belief that ideas are innate, experiences—through the filter of our senses—leave an imprint on our mind, which then serves as a tool to relate to the world in numerous ways. For example, the infant learns what milk or apple juice is through the experience of taste, recognizes the variety of colors of crayons through sight, and is able to distinguish between a mother's or father's voice through hearing, and so on. For the growing infant, those numerous types of sensory experiences evolve and build up as s/he relates, interacts, and understands the world (Ozmon and Craver 1990).

In the classroom setting, the adage of the teacher saying to her students, "I am here to 'fill' your mind" is what perhaps best explains "blank slate" thinking. That is, the idea of "filling" the student's mind is conducted through the number of experiences the teacher provides for her/his students. Ozmon and Craver (1990) explain it this way: "One might think of the human mind as a kind of computer, and until something is programmed in, one cannot get anything out; consequently, Locke emphasized the idea of placing children in the most desired environment for their education and pointed to the importance of environment in making people what they are" (121).

Despite his emphasis on the notion that the mind is a blank slate, Locke did recognize that children have their own characteristics and temperaments, stressing a humane learning environment. That is, the environment should *not* be a contrived setting where children are forced beyond their readiness level, their natural inclinations, and where corporal punishment or severe talk is a part of the instructional approach. In short, Locke—influenced by Comenius—believed children should be immersed in a learning environment that is enjoyable (Crain 2000). The approach to teaching ought to be one that invites children into a conversation, and not one that is dominated by tiresome lectures.

Furthermore, Locke underscored the importance of paying attention to individual differences, meaning the process of education ought to be a customized effort to meet the varying needs and interests of children. Although deemphasizing a learning environment that is governed by rules, for Locke, however, the principal goal of education is the development of good habits and virtuous living, meaning that good character and self-control trumps the training of the intellect. In that light, learning comes about through associations; through arranged step-by-step processes; through repetition in order to develop behavior and habits; through rewards and punishments (verbal praise and disapproval); and through modeling, all of which established the beginning step of an educational psychology that focuses on developmental processes (Crain 2000; Ozmon and Craver 1990).

In the end, while Locke's idea of the mind being a blank slate may have its place, it does, however, have its limitations or shortcomings in that this viewpoint sees the mind as too passive and dependent on external forces, meaning the mind itself is not an active, innate agent in the formulation of thought (Ozmon and Craver 1990). Despite the critical observation of the latter, for Locke, education ultimately is a process of becoming more fully human, which had an influence on the French philosopher Jean-Jacques Rousseau, the other forerunner of educational developmental psychology (Crain 2000).

JEAN-JACQUES ROUSSEAU (1712–1778)

Born in Switzerland, but spending most of his days in France, Rousseau was a philosopher, composer, writer, and national hero. Rousseau's political philosophy indeed had an impact on the thinking of his followers, who saw a feudal system keeping masses of people in a subjected state, thus stoking the flames of the French Revolution. Particularly highlighted in his work *Emile*, Rousseau expounds on his educational philosophy, agreeing with Locke that children are different from adults, but parts ways with him in that he had no faith in the social environment (Crain 2000; Ozmon and Craver 1990).

For Rousseau, children were born pure, good, and inherently free, but it was society that had a corrupting influence on them. Therefore, Rousseau suggests that the artificiality of formal schooling should not be introduced to youngsters until the age of fifteen. Prior to that age, through the guidance of a tutor, yet finding no need for books, a child can learn through a developmental process that unfolds as a result of the child acting on her/his own impulses, interests, and curiosities, clearly underscoring the critical link between nature and experience and the inherent goodness of children (Crain 2000; Ozmon and Craver 1990).

Rousseau (1921) puts it this way:

> Nature provides for the child's growth in her own fashion, and this should never be thwarted. Do not make him sit still when he wants to run about, nor run when he wants to be quiet. If we did not spoil our children's wills by our blunders their desires would be free from caprice. Let them run, jump, and shout to their heart's content. All their own activities are instincts of the body for its growth in strength . . . Hold childhood in reverence, and do not be in any hurry to judge it for good or ill. Leave exceptional cases to show themselves, let their qualities be tested and confirmed, before special methods are adopted. Give nature time to work before you take over her business, lest you interfere with her dealings. You assert that you know the value of time and are afraid to waste it. You fail to perceive that it is a greater waste of time to use it ill than to do nothing, and that a child ill taught is further from virtue than a child who has learnt nothing at all. You are afraid to see him spending his early years doing nothing. What! is it nothing to be happy, nothing to run and jump all day? He will never be so busy again all his life long. (48–68)

What the above suggests is that Rousseau believed that from childhood to adulthood one progresses along in stages, underscoring the idea that growth is a developmental process that is intrinsically and biologically dictated.

This means that according to the plan of nature (or a process of biological maturation), children, for the most part, grow and learn on their own as opposed to being taught by environmental influences, that is, what is taught by the teacher or any other external force. To that end, Rousseau saw the mind as a unique organism with its own innate patterns of thinking and acting, growing and learning through experiences and interaction with the world. In a very real way, Rousseau promoted what is contemporarily referred to as a "child-centered" philosophy of education (Crain 2000).

In the final analysis, the philosophies of Locke and Rousseau have had a notable influence on what we today call educational psychology, branching out into two broad, but sometimes, interrelated threads of thought. For Locke, based on the assumption that the mind is a "blank slate" and that external forces (the environment) impact learning—with the employment of modeling, association, repetition, and the incorporation of rewards (approval) and punishments (disapproval)—we see the thread of what is known as behaviorism emerge. For Rousseau, with the notion that children learn through stages and are natural learners, we see the thread of what is known as developmentalism appear.[2]

Under the umbrella of these two broad threads, which in unison have significantly contributed to child/developmental psychology, the implications are clear as they relate to behaviorism, cognitivism, and humanism, the themes of the following chapter.

NOTES

1. Bacon's work comes out of the philosophical tradition of realism, which is a complex philosophy that has evolved into several varieties of its meaning, all of which are grounded in the notion *"that reality, knowledge, and value exist independent of the human mind"* (Ozmon and Craver 1990, 38, author's emphasis). To put another way, reality or things exists whether they are noticed, acknowledged, or examined (e.g., a flower has always been a flower even before it was formally labeled a flower, or as depicted in that contemporary television commercial, a tree crashing down in the forest still makes a sound whether the sound is humanly acknowledged or not). For Bacon, in an effort to examine reality, it is through inductive reasoning that enables one to gain knowledge in order to interpret the world. The idea of inductive thinking, therefore, begins by the collection of observable particulars, which in the consistency of the collection of those particulars or data, generalities can then be made (Ozmon and Craver 1990). For example, if person after person slips on a banana peel, then the generality can be made to not walk on a banana peel; otherwise, one risks falling down.

2. To be sure, for both Locke and Rousseau, their theories were not without contradictions or inconsistencies. For example, while Locke recognized the natural curiosities or predispositions for children to learn, the notion of behavioristic practices of external rewards/punishments ought not to be necessary in order to steer motivation. In the case of Rousseau, his personal life was one that was riddled with upheaval and questionable decisions, including the abandonment of his five children, sending them to a state home. It was this action, among others, that led many to not even consider Rousseau's thought on child development and education (Crain 2000).

SEVENTEEN

An Overview of Behaviorism, Cognitivism, and Humanism

A theory of development deals with change over time and is usually concerned with three things. First, it should describe changes over time within an area or several areas of development. Second, it should describe changes among areas of development. Finally, it should explain those changes.

(Aldridge and Goldman 2002, 69)

When it comes to educational psychology, concepts related to behaviorism, cognitivism, and humanism greatly inform our understanding of child development, different ways of how we learn, and approaches that can be taken in order to make meaningful connections with students. This chapter discusses these various theoretical concepts, beginning with behaviorism.

BEHAVIORISM

Behaviorism holds the belief that the shaping of behavior and the setting of a climate for one to learn is dictated by stimuli, through the use of rewards and punishments or negative and positive reinforcements, that is, stimulus-response (S-R) theories. Sparking the advent of what is known as classical conditioning, it was Russian physiologist Ivan Pavlov (1849–1936) in his famous experiment to condition dogs whereby he rang a bell (neutral stimulus) every time he brought the dogs food (nonneutral stimulus), causing them to salivate (natural response) (Parkay and Hass 2000; Ozmon and Craver 1990).

The dogs, therefore, came to associate the sound of the bell with the food, which prompted the consistent natural response of salivation. Once this association was established, the dogs were conditioned so much so that the sound of the bell would make them salivate, whether there was food or not. Pavlov's work was simplistic in its conclusions, arguing that conditioning is more about instinctive reflex behavioral responses to external forces devoid of a cognitive process (Parkay and Hass 2000; Ozmon and Craver 1990). Yet Pavlov's pioneering work placed in motion the critical thought of others, such as John B. Watson (1878–1958), E. L. Thorndike (1874–1949), B. F. Skinner (1904–1990), and Albert Bandura (1925–).

Referred to as *Type S* conditioning, classical conditioning was fully embraced by Watson, who rejected the notion that the examination of consciousness has a place in psychology, and argued for a science of psychology that assumed that all learning comes about through conditioning. Therefore, in his view, the focus of study should be on the environmental stimuli that impact overt responses, behaviors, and habits. For example, an infant learns to love his/her mother through the conditioning of the mother, who regularly smiles, rocks, and takes care of the baby (Crain 2000).

Indeed, it was Watson's study of emotions such as fear, love, and rage that suggested that emotions can be conditioned positively or negatively, depending on the stimuli that is evoked (Crain 2000). In capturing the essence of his belief, Watson (1970) memorably claimed:

> Give me a dozen healthy infants, well-formed, and my own specified world to bring them up in and I'll guarantee to take any one at random and train him to become any type of specialist I might select—doctor, lawyer, artist, merchant-chief and, yes, even beggar-man and thief, regardless of his talents, penchants, tendencies, abilities, vocations, and race of his ancestors. (104)

Watson's work not only had an impact on the thinking of Thorndike, who argued that things exist because their existence can be measured, but also on that of Skinner, who claimed an operant conditioning paradigm or *Type R* conditioning. The notion of operant conditioning functions through a system of pleasant (reinforcers) and unpleasant (punishers) consequences in order to control behavior (Slavin 2000; Ozmon and Craver 1990).

In other words, the pleasant reinforces appropriate behavior, and unpleasant punishers weaken inappropriate behavior, all of which underlies the chief assumption that drives behavioral learning theory. While Bandura was influenced by behaviorist theory, he observed that the idea of behavior being shaped by modeling or imitation was essentially ignored, prompting him to examine the impact of social cues on behavior, which has evolved into what is now known as social learning theory, discussed in chapter 19 (Slavin 2000).

In the end, behaviorism is about shaping and directing behavior, and whether that comes about through imitation or the administering of rewards or punishments, its goal is to prompt observable and measurable evidence of that shaping, qualitatively void of interest in the cognitive and conscious nature of our being, a matter acutely noticed by a cognitivist perspective.

COGNITIVISM

Particularly drawing from the work of Jean Piaget (1896–1980), Lev Vygotsky (1896–1934), Erik Erikson (1902–1994), and others, cognitive theory argues that learning moves from the inside out, is developmental, and is engineered through the making of mental connections. In other words, unlike a behaviorist point of view where learning is viewed as a process of transmission dictated by external forces, cognitive theory sees learning as a process of construction regarding how the learner organizes, remembers, and utilizes knowledge (Ryan and Cooper 2013; Slavin 2000).

As Skinner can be considered the "father" of modern behaviorism, Piaget can be characterized as the "father" of cognitivism. Viewing learning as a developmental process, Piaget suggested that from birth to adulthood, human beings pass through stages toward growth by exploring and interacting with the world, constructing new knowledge and information along the way. In other words, children don't so much learn from direct instruction or other external forces, but rather it is their interaction and making sense of their environment in which cognitive growth occurs (Crain 2000). Hence, learning occurs from the inside out.

William Crain (2000) provides a succinct but rich description of Piaget's work as it relates to his conception of the general periods of development (113):

> Period I. Sensori-Motor Intelligence (birth to 2 years). Babies organize their physical action schemes, such as sucking, grasping, and hitting, for dealing with the immediate world.
>
> Period II. Preoperational Thought (2–7 years). Children learn to think—to use symbols and internal images—but their thinking is unsystematic and illogical. It is very different from that of adults.
>
> Period III. Concrete Operations (7–11 years). Children develop the capacity to think systematically, but only when they can refer to concrete objects and activities.
>
> Period IV. Formal Operations (11 to adulthood). Young people develop the capacity to think systematically on a purely abstract and hypothetical plane.

Although Piaget suggests that all people go through each of the defined periods of development, the rate of that development may vary from person to person.

Moreover, as one goes through those stages or periods, the process is inherently steered by one's natural desire to understand their world in what Piaget (1959, 1952) characterizes as a state of equilibrium. Through a process of organization and adaptation, experiences are filtered through schemes (network system in the brain) in order to guide understanding, and to understand through that network is to attain equilibrium.

Lack of understanding causes disequilibrium, which is the prompting force that impacts an adjustment in thinking or development. In other words, this ongoing dynamic is a cognitive activity of *adaptation* whereby the reciprocal processes of *accommodation* and *assimilation* aid the mental schemes to negotiate with the experience in order to maintain equilibrium (Eggen and Kauchak 2004).

For example, consider the child who has learned her numbers one through ten, but later is introduced to counting to fifty. In accommodating this new concept, the child has to make adaptations in his/her existing math scheme, creating a new scheme as a result of the experience, which tells the child that to count one must go beyond the number ten. In other words, in the child's math scheme (counting to ten), a modification is made with the creation of counting to fifty.

Working in concert with the process of accommodation, assimilation, therefore, is a form of adaptation in which an experience is assimilated into an existing scheme. That is, once the child has learned the counting-to-fifty math scheme, s/he likely will grasp that counting is an endeavor that continues, and still later that numbers can be manipulated through concrete operations.

Consider also another example: suppose a ten-year-old child wants to build a bird house. At first, s/he just estimates the size of the wall needed by sight and cuts a piece of wood that s/he thinks will fit. But when s/he puts in the new piece of wood, s/he notices it is too small. S/he is puzzled. Things didn't come about as expected and s/he doesn't know what to do. The child is in a state of disequilibrium and must make adjustments, accommodations. Then s/he decides to actually measure the size that is needed before sawing again. The failure of his/her former approach—just estimating by sight—is replaced by a new method: measuring first. In this way the child develops a new, more effective way of doing things.

In light of the two examples above, and particularly relevant to educators, children need to go through periods of disequilibrium—not knowing—in order to come up with new schemes and ideas. Ignorance, in this sense, is helpful. At the same time, it's best when the problems aren't too far beyond the current stage. Problems should be just a little bit beyond the current capacities. Eggen and Kauchak (2004) assert that:

> When considering how organization and adaptation lead to cognitive development, an important principle must be kept in mind: *All growth depends on existing schemes*; a scheme is never formed in isolation . . . This principle is one of the most important contributions of Piaget's developmental theory. It suggests that teachers should select and present topics that build on learners' current understanding and disrupt equilibrium enough to be motivating but not overwhelming. (39)

While Piaget argued that children were intrinsically motivated and that development is the antecedent for learning, Vygotsky saw learning as one preceding and leading development in a culturally, socially, and linguistically contextualized setting (Casbergue 2013; Eggen and Kauchak 2004).

Therefore, development best occurs through social interaction between peers, though guided by a more knowledgeable adult who fosters a learning setting that asks prompting questions, always working within the learner's zone of proximal development (to be later explained). For Vygotsky, the role of language was critical to his theory, which assumes that by interacting with others, language provides a gateway to knowledge; is a cognitive tool that aids thinking; and serves as a mechanism to reflect and regulate thinking (Casbergue 2013; Eggen and Kauchak 2004). And, as Crain (2000) points out, while Vygotsky did not use the term *metacognition*—one's awareness of one's thinking—he was a pioneering agent in bringing to light this important concept. Awareness of what we think and how we think aids in controlling or regulating our thinking.

Erikson, while technically not a cognitive theorist but a psychoanalyst who was interested in the ego's cognitive functions, is particularly recognized for his contribution to what is known as psychosocial theory, which examines development through the integration of personal, emotional, and social elements. With the assumption that human beings generally possess similar basic needs, and to the degree of the quality of those met needs as determined by the care and support of the social environment, the impact is manifested either favorably or adversely on how one personally develops (Eggen and Kauchak 2004).

This development unfolds through a series of stages: *Trust Versus Mistrust (birth to one year); Autonomy Versus Shame and Doubt (Ages one to three); Initiative Versus Guilt (ages three to six); Industry Versus Inferiority (ages six to twelve); Identity Versus Confusion (ages twelve to eighteen); Intimacy Versus Isolation (young adulthood); Generativity Versus Stagnation (middle adulthood);* and *Integrity Versus Despair (old age).* While one can examine in detail elsewhere the various aspects of each stage, the shortcomings in Erikson's theory, among other limitations, are based on the fact that he drew his conclusions on his work with males, and he did not consider cultural context when making generalities. Yet the strength of his theory is that environment matters, and for teachers in particular, the setting and fostering of a positive, nurturing, and caring environment are critical toward building a healthy self-concept for children (Eggen and Kauchak 2004).

HUMANISM

Humanistic thought has a long history, dating back to the ancient traditions of both Eastern and Western philosophies, espousing a variety of perspectives, yet with the common thread that focuses on the inherent goodness of human beings. And humanistic psychology has a focus on the development of the whole person, our motivation, and how we can reach our full potential. In other words, for educators, humanism is a point of view that collectively is mindful of the psychological, emotional, physical, intellectual, and interpersonal needs of each of their students, providing a sense of belonging (Pugach 2006; Eggen and Kauchak 2004).[1]

Abraham Maslow (1908–1970) stands out as the preeminent leader of the contemporary humanistic movement, highlighted with his well-known hierarchy of needs paradigm (Eggen and Kauchak 2004, 354):

Deficiency Needs
Survival (shelter, warmth, food, water)
Safety (freedom from physical or emotional threat)
Belonging (love and acceptance from family and peers)
Self-esteem (recognition and approval)

Growth Needs
Intellectual achievement (knowing and understanding)
Aesthetic appreciation (order, truth, beauty)
Self-actualization

According to Maslow, upon the meeting of needs, beginning with the deficiency needs being met and continuing thereafter with subsequent needs being met, an individual can move forward toward the satisfying-of-the-growth needs.

There is an obvious certain merit in Maslow's theory. For example, children have been known to come to school hungry. Hunger is an unsatisfied need, negatively impacting motivation for a child to concentrate on school work. The implementation of school breakfast/lunch programs assumes the hunger need will be met; therefore, the child is motivated to do school work. Yet the idea of needs being a hierarchal matter defies adults and even children who, despite the odds, have lived under the threat of hunger, safety, and belonging, yet still were resilient enough to achieve a level of self-actualization.

Carl Rogers (1902–1987), Haim Ginott (1922–1973), and Rollo May (1909–1994), among others, also stand out as critical thinkers who have contributed to humanistic psychology, emphasizing the being, the inside of an individual as a happening to be nurtured, explored, and validated. Therefore, in order to foster motivation, healthy relationships, and an overall positive classroom environment, Eggen and Kauchak (2004) rightly suggest that educators consider the following (356):

- Treat students as people first and students second.
- Provide students with unconditional positive regard by separating their behaviors from their intrinsic worth.
- Create safe and orderly classrooms where students believe they can learn and where they are expected to do so.
- Consider teaching-learning experiences from students' points of view.

In the end, the glue that is educational psychology works to greatly inform and ground educators on how they pedagogically approach their diverse student population.[2] Section V further expands what is highlighted in this section, importantly making its link to the five components of knowledge.

NOTES

1. Humanistic psychology largely emerged as a response to the theories of behaviorism, and drawing from the developmental tradition, its focus on the forces that impact inner growth discernibly adds to the body of knowledge that contributes to educational psychology (Crain 2000).

2. This introductory overview of educational psychology highlighted in section IV and the emphasis on the work of several of its notable contributors simply scratches the surface of their thought, notwithstanding the work of still many others who have significantly contributed to theoretically explaining human behavior, development, and how learning unfolds. For example, see the work of Crain (2000), who in detail discusses the work of Arnold Gesell (maturational theory), Lawrence Kohlberg (moral development), Sigmund Freud (psychoanalytic theory), and Noam Chomsky (language development) among others. The point here, of course, is to underscore the overall importance of educational psychology as a collective body of thought that requires significant exploration, and that richly informs the knowledge base of teachers and maximizes their efforts in working with a diverse student population.

Section V

Five Components of Knowledge

Classrooms are complex because events tend to overlap: Many things happen at once, and they happen quickly.

(Guillaume 2004, 1)

EIGHTEEN
Knowledge of Pedagogy and Knowledge of Classroom Management

> *Great teachers intentionally arrange, rearrange, alter, and adjust the structures that frame their teaching.*
>
> (Whitaker 2004, 85)

The defining mark of the effectiveness of teachers is established by how knowledgeable they are, which here is inclusive of five separate, but interrelated, components: knowledge of students, knowledge of subject matter, knowledge of pedagogy, knowledge of learning, and knowledge of classroom management. And to reiterate, as thematically suggested throughout the chapters in section IV, the oxygen that breathes life into each of these interrelated components is educational psychology. The focus of this chapter is centered on the first two components, with the following chapter highlighting the remaining three.

KNOWLEDGE OF PEDAGOGY

The term "pedagogy" signifies the art and science of teaching, which is concretely expressed through the instructional approach taken by the teacher. The suggested difference, therefore, between pedagogy and instruction implies that the concept *pedagogy* is driven by a point of view, a belief system, a philosophy of teaching, and *instruction* is the carrying out of that philosophy in action (Koch 2009).

Hence, based on one's philosophy of teaching and learning, instructional approaches are fundamentally determined by taking into account the grade level being taught, the background knowledge of students, pupil–teacher ratio, cultural considerations, subject matter being taught/discussed, available resources/material, and time frame given. This denotes that instruction is not a dynamic that is led by one's seat-of-the-pants impulses, but rather one that is coordinated by preparation, awareness of objectives and purposes, is contextually linked, realizes the necessity of varied strategies (i.e., one size does not fit all), all of which has as its goal to meaningfully engage students in the teaching and learning act.

In short, instruction is a thoughtful endeavor that is grounded by one's pedagogical philosophy, which is filtered through the autobiographical nature of teaching (see chapter 13). The point here, however, is not so much to discuss how to write a useful lesson plan or explain specific instructional strategies, but rather to provide an overview of three models that generally drive classroom instruction, of which all teachers ought to be aware. These approaches are deductive (direct), inductive (indirect), and integrated.

Deductive (Direct) Instructional Model

One might refer to direct instruction as a "teacher-centered" instructional approach, largely driven by a mindset that the student comes to the class as a "blank slate," where it is the task of the teacher to fill the student's mind with the content being studied. In general, therefore, the classroom environment is systematically directed by the teacher, letting students know what the objective of the lesson is, then proceeding to present the information or content, typically in a lecture format that is sequential and straightforward in nature, particularly concerning itself with what the outcome or final product will be as a result of the lesson (Guillaume 2004).

For example, in a second-grade class lesson on nouns, the teacher may begin the lesson by saying, "Boys and girls, today we will learn what a noun is, " and then explain what a noun is, providing specific examples. After the lesson is over, and perhaps taking questions from students, the teacher then moves the students to do independent work, working toward, in this case, the mastery of nouns.

Direct instruction can be characterized as a "skill and drill" approach with a clear set of material or information that is necessary for all students to learn. However, this approach ought to be used with caution in that the teacher centeredness of the entire dynamic can easily cultivate student passivity, boredom, and disconnection (Guillaume 2004; Slavin 2000). In short, direct instruction is an "approach to teaching in which the teacher transmits information directly to the students; lessons are goal-orientated and structured by the teacher" (Slavin 2000, 220).

Inductive (Indirect) Instructional Model

In an inductive instructional approach, unlike a direct approach that is explicitly teacher centered, the teacher acts more as a facilitator, engaging students in examining data, material, and concepts. While mindful of final outcome of the lesson, teaching inductively is interested in process, tapping into student interests and curiosities as the students move to learn through discovery (Guillaume 2004). Whereas a deductive approach moves from whole to part, an inductive approach moves from part to whole.

For example, the second-grade class scenario of the lesson on nouns was explicit regarding the topic to be learned, was then directly taught, and was subsequently practiced. In an inductive approach, however, the teacher may begin the lesson by asking the students: Who likes pizza? What city do we live in? Who has a pet? There are numerous other types of questions the students can easily and enthusiastically respond to.

Engaging the students in this manner not only demonstrates an interest in students and their lives, but also naturally leads students to that place where they are talking about persons, places, and things, that is, nouns. To be sure, there are multiple strategies and approaches to inductive instruction, all of which logically fall under a constructivist learning rubric, which encourages participation, active learning, and generally begins a lesson "with a question, a case, or a problem" (Cooperstein and Kocevar-Weidinger 2004, 142).

Largely attributed to the work of Jean Piaget, the notion of constructivism is driven by what can be characterized as a "student-centered" approach to teaching and learning.[1] The assumption is that the more the teacher draws from the children's existing experience and knowledge base, the likelihood of captivating their interest and drawing them into authentically learning something new is far greater than having the children sit in a classroom where they are passive recipients, simply being taught deductively and learning through memorization, skill, and drill (Kirylo 2011). In other words, as Cooperstein and Kocevar-Weidinger (2004) argue, a constructivist approach allows one to construct meaning that becomes one's own, often coming in social settings where ideas and concepts are exchanged.[2]

The central important positive aspect to an inductive instructional approach is that it places students at the center of the teaching and learning act, where the possibility of their engagement with the process is great. To teach in an inductive way clearly requires the teacher to be well versed in various constructivist approaches, such as the incorporation of cooperative learning groups, learning through discovery (e.g., experiments and critical-thinking-related activities), and other types of student-centered strategies. The vulnerability of inductive instruction is dictated by the teacher's preparation, theoretical knowledge, time, and understanding as to when and how to meaningfully incorporate the approach.

Integrated Model Approach: Differentiated Instruction (DI)

Informed by brain-based learning theory, sociocultural theory, multiple intelligences theory, a differentiated instructional (DI) approach is driven by the assumption that the need of the student drives the instruction, assuring the approach is developmentally appropriate and draws from a variety of best practices in order to maximize the possibility of student learning (Burkett 2013; Wormeli 2005).

In other words, as Tomlinson (2013) argues, DI is not a roadmap providing teachers specific instructional strategies; rather, DI is a way of thinking and planning, being mindful of the unpredictable nature inherently enmeshed in the teaching and learning process. Guided by the notion of respectful teaching, "at its most basic level, differentiating instruction means *'shaking up'* what goes on in the classroom so that students have multiple options for taking in information, making sense of ideas, and expressing what they learn" (Tomlinson 2013, 3).

Indeed, DI views difference as a strength, realizing students enter the classroom door from a variety of backgrounds, interest levels, school-readiness levels, gifts, talents, strengths, limitations, and weaknesses. Accordingly, the task of the teacher is to thoughtfully plan for difference relative to the content (what students are to learn), process (activities involved to foster learning), and product (capstone projects/artifacts indicative of learning). While the content serves as the destination point, it does not have as its goal to "cover the curriculum," but rather is driven by a common sense, nurturing, and flexible environment—that has as its goal student learning and satisfaction in that learning, which can be assessed through culminating types of projects (Tomlinson 2014).

In this light, DI can be characterized as an integrated approach to teaching and learning, whereby the approach can be conducted through a deductive or inductive paradigm, or a combination of both, realizing students have different needs and learn differently. While it is beyond the scope of purpose here to discuss the practicalities or the "how" of DI, to teach with a DI model in mind, it is clear the teacher needs to be well prepared, possess a deep understanding of the theory that drives her thinking and action, and manage time well.[3]

KNOWLEDGE OF CLASSROOM MANAGEMENT

Not only does teaching require a command of subject matter as well as a deep understanding of how to teach and how one learns, it also requires one to have adept classroom-management skills, which fosters an engaging learning environment. Informed by educational psychology, classroom management takes thoughtful preparation and is guided by a way of thinking about one's diverse student population.

Carried out by strategies that cultivate an orderly climate, the action of classroom management is punctuated with respect for student differences and managing time well, is caring, and is proactive in working toward student growth. Moreover, classroom management includes the maintaining of good records and other necessary housekeeping responsibilities. Finally, discipline, which is a component of classroom management, denotes the approaches that are utilized to prevent, respond to, or reduce inappropriate behaviors (Ryan and Cooper 2013; Slavin 2000).

To that end, the environmental foundation in which classroom management must be filtered is a teacher's thinking, which should be mindful of promoting an education that is developmentally appropriate, suggesting that the instructional approach, the discipline procedures, the curriculum used, and the overall interaction with students are appropriate in order to healthily foster cognitive, social, cultural, physical, and emotional growth. An excellent position paper put out by the National Association for the Education of Young Children (NAEYC 2009) argues that a teacher's knowledge base and decision-making skills are essential to effective classroom practice, emphasizing that teachers must work toward individually knowing their students, to possessing a deep awareness level of child development and learning, and to be aware of the value systems, experiences, and social, cultural, and linguistic forces that have impacted their students' lives—all in order to better serve their diverse student population.

And in that light, and fitting for the purposes here, LaCaze and Kirylo (2012) provide what they characterize as *A Practical Guide to a Principled Classroom* when considering concepts related to classroom management (8–9):

1. Demonstrate a Positive Attitude

[As emphasized in section II of this text], an effective teacher is one who possesses a positive attitude and realizes that education is fundamentally about entering into relationships (Comer 2004). Establishing a meaningful dialogical environment with students and their families aids greatly in building a constructive relational foundation of communication and understanding. Moreover, a critical aspect of a positive learning environment is a stimulating setting where students feel a sense of value and acceptance, all of which ultimately plays a significant role in their growth (Bowman 2007).

2. Expectations Are Clear

It is critical that the teacher begins the academic year by establishing clear expectations regarding classroom behavior. This provides students with a sense of direction, purpose, and an understanding of parameters (Richardson and Fallona 2001). Additionally, the behavior-management plan must be fair and understandable, which helps maintain a productive learning environment and increases the likelihood that students will try to meet those expectations (Charles 2008; Wheeler and Richey 2009).

3. Understandable Rules

Classroom rules and consequences should be written in a concise, logical, and positive way. To avoid multiple interpretations, rules should be specific and clearly visible in the classroom. In addition to students understanding rules and expectations, parents/caregivers must have a clear understanding of them as well. In short, there is a positive impact on student cooperation and achievement when they concretely understand the rules and consequences (Danforth and Boyle 2007).

4. Fairness Is Key

Fairness is key and establishing trust is essential, which implies the teacher is critically aware of cultural differences, individual needs, strengths, weaknesses, and limitations. Regardless of background, every student must be given the opportunity to succeed, which helps maintain a classroom environment that is safe, predictable, and constructive (Santrock 2009; Charles 2008). It is also important to convey that fairness is not a one-size-fits-all approach. That is, students need to be aware that they may not all get the same thing, but rather they will all get what they need.

5. Constructive Consistency Is Fundamental

[As noted in chapter 4, consistency is the other side of the coin of persistence, and] is marked with such concepts as harmony, regularity, and [absence of] contradiction. The manifestation of constructive consistency occurs when students possess a clear, secure, and certain understanding of the appropriate dispositions and actions of the teacher (Kirylo, 2008). Helping to avoid confusion and adherence to rules, constructive consistency provides students with needed boundaries and a sense of safety (Wheeler and Richey 2009).

6. Address Disruptions with as Little Interruption as Possible

When a teacher is faced with classroom disruptions, it is imperative that s/he address them with as little interruption of class momentum as possible. A minor disruption can easily escalate if it is blown out of proportion and not appropriately handled. That is, there are many verbal and nonverbal cues a teacher can employ, while at the same time minimizing the teaching and learning process (i.e., consistently circulating the class as students are working; a stern look; standing next to the student; tapping the student on the shoulder when not on task; positively pointing out the acceptable behavior of those staying on task) (Danforth and Boyle 2007).

7. Avoid Confrontations

A critical point of behavior management is not to confront and engage in a power play; rather the key is to diffuse and for the teacher to stay calm. Moreover, confrontations are uncomfortable for students; therefore, as much as possible, potential volatile situations should be handled discretely in order to avoid embarrassment and resentment. However, if the teacher is not able to immediately control the disruption, the student should be escorted out of the classroom in order to handle the conflict away from other students (Danforth and Boyle 2007). Arguing with a student in front of others sends an undermining message of clarified rules and consequences (Richardson and Fallona 2001).

8. Incorporate Humor

Humor is a powerful tool teachers can utilize in order to facilitate an inviting classroom atmosphere. Additionally, humor helps to establish a relaxed climate and marks the teacher as one who is approachable (Richardson and Fallona 2001). The appropriate use of humor can diffuse a tense situation and aid in releasing pent up negative thinking. As a word of caution, however, humor must not be confused with sarcasm, which is an unacceptable form of communication with students.

9. Overplan

Fundamental to an effective teacher is that s/he is well prepared and anticipates how long lessons will take. In addition, the teacher prepares for individual differences and secures a sufficient amount of materials. Finally, the teacher overplans, and avoids the notion of unplanned "free time," which invites potential student disruption, unnecessary noise, and a waste of valuable learning time. Overplanning plans for free time, implying the teacher has a prepared choice of learning activities for those who complete assignments early (Walker, Shea, and Bauer 2007).

10. Begin Anew Daily

Beginning anew each day signifies that the teacher has a short memory. That is, regardless of the behavior-management challenges of the day before with a certain student(s), the teacher begins each day with a fresh start, a new beginning, always working on hope and persistence that the student(s) will move closer toward the ultimate goal of becoming intrinsically motivated while at the same time taking possession of self-discipline. If students think that the teacher will personally hold their behavior against them, they will begin to lose motivation in the class (Santrock 2009). The concept of beginning anew daily has a tremendous impact on countering the latter.

The critical points highlighted above simply serve as a practical guide in working toward effectively managing a classroom. And the teacher naturally stands as a figure of authority in that setting, but that figurehead does not imply authoritarianism and dictatorship, but rather one who negotiates, empowers, and cultivates student growth.

In that light, a fundamental goal for any classroom-management plan is one that fosters an environment in which students are central in taking intrinsic command of a constructive learning environment. As we move forward to chapter 19, we continue to explore the other three components of knowledge, clearly interrelated to the aforementioned ones.

NOTES

1. Paulo Freire (1921–1997), the Brazilian educator, existential thinker, and social activist, had great respect for Piaget's work and argued that it was impossible to consider the teaching of literacy without drawing from Piaget's thought and that of Lev Vygotsky. Freire also asserted, however, without false modesty, that it is not possible to ponder the notion of constructivism without considering what he contributed to the concept. That is, while Piaget attempted to study cognitive processes as a "neutral" endeavor in his sample sizes of middle-class young people, Freire's notion of constructivism is more political in nature, mindful of the social, cultural, economic, and historical forces at work (Kincheloe 2008; Freire 2007, 1995; Freire and Vittoria 2007).

2. Particularly influenced by the thought of Jean-Jacques Rousseau, the work of Maria Montessori—certainly capturing worldwide popularity—is constructivist in nature, where the teacher acts as facilitator or guide, allowing for free choice, sensitive to the interests and curiosities of children, fostering "their powers of inner construction" (Crain 2000, 69).

3. A large amount of literature exists discussing various strategies, considerations, and approaches as to how to incorporate DI in practice, particularly, among others, to be found in the work of Carol Ann Tomlinson.

NINETEEN
Knowledge of Learning, Knowledge of Students, and Knowledge of Subject Matter

A teacher may be an English teacher, a math teacher, or a history teacher, but she is really a teacher of human beings.

(Ryan 2008, 12)

KNOWLEDGE OF LEARNING

According to Merriam-Webster (2012), to learn is to acquire knowledge, understanding, or skill via a process that comes about through instruction, experience, practice, and study. The act of learning, therefore, is an ownership proposition, which enables a change in one's knowledge or behavior as a result of the learning experience. And this learning experience can be explained through two broad theories called behavioral theory and cognitive theory (Koch 2009; Parkay and Hass 2000).

Behavioral Theory

Also referred to as behaviorism, behavioral theory, as mentioned in chapter 17, suggests that we learn through a stimulus-response (S-R) approach. That is, a learning response can be incentivized by either a pleasurable or unpleasant stimulus that is externally reinforced (Koch 2009; Parkay and Hass 2000; Slavin 2000). A student who receives the A or the F, the smiley face or frowny face, the extra privilege or relegated to "sit in the corner," are only but a few examples that reinforce either pleasurably or not.

In short, guided by concrete objectives, a behaviorist approach is a teacher-directed or teacher-centered event, with the assumption that it will impact learning as measured through observable behavior or outcomes. While there is a place for external incentives in order to prompt learning, it does risk fostering a classroom atmosphere that simply operates through a system of bribery, with the consequence of dulling students' sense of drawing from their internal mechanism that allows for deep thinking and the examination of complex concepts (Koch 2009; Kohn 1999).

Emerging from the principles of behavioral learning theory, social learning theory argues that human beings possess a boundless capacity to learn, only limited by the expectations and behavior cues deemed appropriate by the social environment (e.g., family, peers, school, occupation). In other words, these expectations and cues inform thought, and the processes of that thought inform action, which is a lifelong dynamic that negotiates learning (Parkay and Hass 2000; Slavin 2000; Bandura 1986).

Developed by Albert Bandura, social theory advances the idea of modeling (learning through imitation), vicarious learning (learning as a result of observing the consequences of the behavior of others), and observational learning, a process of learning that includes four phases: attentional phase (grabbing the attention of students through provoking cues, surprise, etc.); retention phase (modeling the desired behavior or action, leaving room for students to practice); reproduction (student practice in order to reproduce the model); and motivational phase (reinforced by grades, approval, or to please the teacher, students are motivated to model behavior or action) (Parkay and Hass 2000; Slavin 2000; Bandura 1986).

Cognitive Learning Theory (Constructing Knowledge)

Slavin (2000) concisely makes the point that "the human mind is a meaning maker" (174). Therefore, as was also underscored in chapter 17, cognitive theory recognizes that learning is a movement from the inside out, is developmental, and suggests that the mind makes meaning through a process of organization, through one's schema or schemata, which is a network of linked facts, ideas, and concepts, implying that learning occurs through a process of construction (Ryan and Cooper 2013; Slavin 2000).

For example, referring back to the previous chapter on an inductive approach to the teaching of nouns, the teacher assumes all her second graders have experienced the eating of pizza, that they realize what city in which they reside, and that some of them may have a pet. These experiences are easily stored in their minds and readily retrievable; hence, this is the reason why the teacher asks what she presumes would draw her students into the lesson. In addition, the students know what the actual words "pizza," "city," and "pet" look like.

That network of information is stored in their schemata or background knowledge. The teacher is thus facilitating an environment where the students then take what they know and then constructively link it to the new knowledge (i.e., nouns). Unlike the idea that students enter the classroom door as a "blank slate," the notion of constructivism assumes that students enter the classroom door with background knowledge, experiences, curiosities, and interests.

In order to guide students to make conceptual connections between what they know and what they need to learn, the teacher acts more like a facilitator, realizing that students may be in need of "scaffolding" (i.e., guidance, support). A concept developed by Lev Vygotsky, scaffolding can occur through a teacher, peer, parent, and so on, where the student is working within a zone of proximal development. That zone is the place where the student is able or is capable of doing a task, but with assistance (scaffolding) in order to reach that place of learning (Slavin 2000; Vygotsky 1978).[1]

And while Vygotsky certainly embraced Jean Piaget's concept of schema theory, he also emphasized that learning is not a solitary event of construction, but one that takes into consideration the social context, emphasizing that youngsters learn through social interactions. This important concept is what gave rise to the idea of setting up classroom cooperative working groups, which assumes that learning takes place through social interaction (Koch 2009; Vygotsky 1962).

However learning takes place in a classroom setting that is constructivist in nature, the idea of moving students to discover knowledge on their own is part of that process, which forces them to critically think, to make connections, and to ultimately learn something new. Hence, discovery learning, an idea that comes out of the work of Jerome Bruner, places a great responsibility on students to actively learn (Koch 2009). To be sure, a classroom setting where a constructivist approach is evident is a classroom that houses a well-informed, prepared, and enthusiastic teacher.

Multiple Intelligence Theory

Multiple intelligence theory posits that human beings can potentially exhibit intelligence in several different ways: linguistic, logical-mathematical, musical, spatial, bodily-kinesthetic, interpersonal, intrapersonal, naturalist, and existential (Gardner 2000, 1983).

The critical strength in grasping the meaning and intent of this theory lies in the fact that students enter the classroom door with various gifts, talents, interests, and curiosities, implying that teachers and school systems in general not only work toward providing a varied curricula approach, but also work toward maximizing efforts to tap into and cultivate students' natural proclivities and intelligences. While this theory is somewhat empirically lacking and does not fully address the relationship between intelligence and our networked memory system (Eggen and Kauchak 2004; Guillaume 2004), it is one, however, that has opened wide the conversation of not viewing intelligence in a reductionist way.

In the final analysis, as we consider how one teaches, the approach is also impacted by an understanding of learning styles. This implies that we all learn or absorb information differently simply dictated by experiences, cultural considerations, and numerous other factors. Indeed, the three discussed components of knowledge are certainly contingent on the fact that teachers work to get to know their students and possess a command of the subject matter in order to best maximize the possibilities of learning.

KNOWLEDGE OF STUDENTS

Knowledge of students, or getting to know one's students, is about entering into healthy working relationships with them. It is the quality of the relationships that are established that determines the likelihood of meaningful learning to occur.

A teacher cannot know a student's strengths, weaknesses, shortcomings, interests, frustration level, or what makes that student tick or what lulls them away, what instills, provokes, or inspires—without getting to know the student. To be sure, knowing one's student is elemental in linking the five interrelated components of knowledge. For a further discussion on knowledge of students, refer back to section II.

KNOWLEDGE OF SUBJECT MATTER

Teachers obviously need to possess knowledge of the subject matter they are to teach, which naturally begins in their formative years of K–12 education, but most formally comes about as a result of attending a quality teacher-education program where subject-matter specialization is a critical aspect of its program (and later to be maintained through ongoing professional development).

However—as important as that may be—knowledge of subject matter is only one aspect of this component, meaning that enthusiasm or passion for teaching the particular discipline is another aspect signifying one's disposition toward the subject matter and its impact on how it is delivered to students. As Ball and McDiarmid (1990) assert, "whether or not they intend to, teachers in all subjects influence students through their own engagement in ideas and processes. Teachers' intellectual resources and dispositions largely determine their capacity to engage students' minds and hearts in learning" (439).

To put it another way, a deep understanding of the particular subject matter to be taught also means making it accessible for students, suggesting that the teacher is aware of student background, experiences, prior knowledge, and that the teacher understands what is involved in the process of learning.[2] Moreover, this implies that the teacher has a confident command of the subject matter, that s/he is able to be flexible with it, and is clear about its connection to other disciplines and everyday life (Hammerness et al. 2005; Darling-Hammond 1997). In other words, s/he sees the process of learning the subject matter as a meaning-making endeavor as opposed to a meaning-inheriting enterprise (Fecho 2011).

NOTES

1. Vygotsky (1978) describes the zone of proximal development as "the distance between the actual developmental level as determined by independent problem solving and the level of potential development as determined through problem solving under adult guidance or in collaboration with more capable peers" (86).

2. A deep understanding of subject matter and its intersection with awareness of student background knowledge of course refers to both the regular-education and special-education population. The special-education population, which is approximately 13 percent (6.4 million) of enrolled public-school students in the United States, is comprised of students with a variety of disabilities: speech/language, hearing, emotional, orthopedic, visual, autism, deaf-blindness, traumatic brain injury, developmentally delayed, among others (National Center for Education Statistics n.d.). To be sure, teachers working with the special-needs population must be uniquely qualified in their knowledge of learning, knowledge of students, and knowledge of subject matter.

Section VI

Assessment Is to "Sit With"

Not everything that can be counted counts, and not everything that counts can be counted.

(Cameron 1963, 13)

TWENTY
Two Different Processes

Assessment and Evaluation

> *Assessment alone is more of a clinical look at performance, its characteristics, its strengths and weaknesses. However, in an evaluation we make a further judgment as to whether such a profile is good or bad in light of institutional or personal expectations.*
>
> (Wiggins 1998, 192–93)

There is the familiar cartoon illustration where a young child named "Mary" is standing with her dog sitting next to her, and she says to another child, "I taught my dog to read." Intrigued, the other child gives the dog a book to read and bellows, "read, Fido, read." But the dog does not read the passage, prompting the child to question, "I thought you said you taught your dog to read?" Mary sharply responds, declaring, "I said I taught my dog to read, but I didn't say he learned to read." This brief illustration strikes to the heart of assessment, which is the other side of the coin of teaching. In other words, how is it that we come to know that students are learning?

Wiggins (1993) reminds us that the etymology of the word "assess" comes from the Latin verb *assidere*, to "sit with," making the implications clear. That is, the idea of assessment in a school setting, as Wiggins explains, is not something teachers do to students, but rather an activity that they do with and for the students. In the simple, albeit far-out example above, Mary indeed engaged in the act of "teaching," but since Fido was not even close to being a part of the process, the dog did not learn to read.

It is not uncommon for teachers to be engrossed in the act of teaching, but if students are not active in the process of "sitting" with the teacher, the likelihood of meaningful learning to occur falls to the wayside. Moreover, the idea of assessment is very different from the idea of testing. Further making the point, Wiggins (1993) puts it this way: "The assessor tries to ferret out all of what the student knows and can do by various means. The tester, on the other hand, demands of the student specific responses to fixed questions of the tester's choosing" (16).

The idea of being assessor, therefore, not only assumes that one possesses a deep understanding of why s/he assesses, when s/he assesses, and how s/he assesses in order to impact student learning in positive and constructive ways, but also the stance is one that is viewed through a lens of inquiry, collaboratively working with students, and depends on varying forms of assessments in order to make adjustments as needed to maximize the teaching and learning process (NTCE 2013). In short, educational assessment is the systematic process of gathering information, data, and happenings that are occurring in the classroom.

This gathering can be collected for an individual or a group, and can be conducted through a variety of means and for a variety of purposes. For example, to name a few, assessments can come in the form reflective observations, interviews, teacher-constructed tests, standardized tests, portfolio type systems, and rubrics, and can be administered in a formative and summative manner. Whereas formative assessments are ongoing types of monitoring feedback constructs (e.g., quizzes, assignments, observations), summative assessments are those that are the sum of the parts (e.g., final exam, project, culminating event, standardized tests).

EVALUATION

Different from the meaning of assessment, evaluation is the process of making value judgments on the formative or summative gathered information, data, and happenings. Whether these judgments come in the form of verbal or written narratives, grades, standardized scores, or a combination of the three, evaluations can be conducted formally or informally. For the latter, a teacher who may have a telephone conversation with a parent about how her/his child did that day in school would be an example of an informal evaluative activity. And for the former, a child going home with his/her nine-week report card grades in which the parent must view and then sign the document for verification is an example of a formal evaluation.

Either way—informally or formally—the idea of passing judgments (evaluations) is an action that assigns value to an event, individual, object or process, making this a philosophical endeavor on how to appropriately weigh the placing of value to whatever is being evaluated (Marsh and Willis 2007).

In that light, therefore, the idea of evaluating critically considers the merit and worth of the evaluand (i.e., the person, object, or activity being evaluated). As the two pieces of value, *merit*, on the one hand, is a context-free piece, meaning the entity possesses intrinsic value in itself. On the other hand, *worth* is the piece that is contextually determined. For example, gold has inherent, aesthetic value in itself, but its worth is contingent on the fluctuations of the market (Lincoln and Guba 1980).

From an evaluative perspective on curricula decisions, as another example, the idea of a required course of study of indigenous languages in Australia as part of the core curriculum in a tenth-grade class in Iowa certainly has merit, but its worth is dubious in relationship to all the other courses and activities students are required to take in the state of Iowa.

Finally, as mentioned above, the nine-week report card grades certainly have merit—even more so—the end-of-year report card grades clearly have merit, but their contextual worth with respect to high-stakes test scores is clearly up for debate, particularly during this current education political climate.

Indeed, as Lincoln and Guba (1980) put it, worth "cannot be established without an intimate knowledge of local social, cultural, political, and value factors" (61). To be sure, when it comes to evaluation and the kinds of assessments instruments that are used, the notion of placing value judgments is contextual, can be complicated, and can be a difficult process to fully and fairly put into place.

In fact, when it comes to conversations about education, concepts related to assessment is arguably the number-one politically laden and heated issue intersecting the social, cultural, psychological, pedagogical, curricula-related, political, and economical domains. To that end, the following chapter provides the historical unfolding of assessment that has led to where we are in practice in school today. Subsequent chapters then further explore the challenges, and where we ought to go moving forward.

TWENTY-ONE
The Emergence of a Testing Movement

> *The assessment movement can trace its origins to the intellectual movement known as postmodernism. . . . The testing movement started just after World War I. In order to understand the big picture of assessment, it is necessary to go back even further to the 1880s.*
>
> (Janesick 2001, 89)

As an advocate for the science of education, John Dewey viewed this science as one that intertwined psychology, philosophy, and sociology, all of which suggested the study of education as a social science (Lagemann 2000). Indeed, for Dewey and the progressive education movement, teaching is an endeavor in which the teacher thoughtfully considers the background of the child, his/her experiences, gifts, talents, and interests in light of the teacher's knowledge of subject matter, methods, and students. In other words, Dewey cultivated the idea of the teacher as a professional and one who was empowered "that would make teaching more individually responsive rather than more formulaic" (Darling-Hammond 2006b, 77).

However, Edward L. Thorndike (1874–1949), a psychologist and one who held the "science" of education in a very different light from his contemporary Dewey, comes from the behaviorist school, arguing that the science of education makes its relevance when it can be precisely measured. To underscore that difference in even stronger terms, Thorndike has been purported to claim he did not understand Dewey and viewed his educational writings as primitive (Lagemann 2000).

Dubbed as the "father of the measurement movement," Thorndike viewed the mind as a physiological object in which his educational studies "favored precise, numerical measurements of anything and everything relevant to education—mental capacities, changes in behavior, and even the aims of education" (Lagemann 2000, 57–59). To be sure early on in the twentieth century, the proverbial educational lines in the sand were drawn with two distinct streams of thought, resulting in what Lagemann (2000) characterizes as Thorndike's triumph and Dewey's defeat.

That is, while Dewey has been extraordinarily influential on educational thought and practice and perhaps even misunderstood over the years, when it comes to viewing education as science and its link to psychology and the "measuring" of students, Thorndike's strand of influence—albeit highly controversial—appears to have had more of a politically influential effect up to this day.[1] To that end, to understand assessment as it is practiced today, a quick trip back in time would be helpful.

A PEEK BACK IN TIME

All teachers are likely familiar with what is known as the Socratic "method," an approach to teaching that fosters a classroom climate that engages students in thoughtful dialogue through a reflective inquiry type of approach. Indeed, this way of teaching dates back to fourth-century Greece where Socrates engaged his students in discussion, assessing along the way not so much on the rightness or wrongness of their responses, but rather how the dialogue took them to a deeper level of critical thought and knowledge (Mathews 2006). To put it another way, as Johnson and Reed (2008) highlight, the irony of the Socratic approach is that one realizes "the educated person is precisely the person who knows her or his limitations, who knows that she or he does not know" (23).

With respect to the advent of assessment tools that were more standardized in nature, China emerges as the earliest in recorded history to administer them over two thousand years ago (Black 1998), and with the invention of the printing press in Europe in 1450, the increased use of written exams was evident (Mathews 2006). Prior to 1840, however, in early American education, testing generally implied oral examinations.[2] But as the common school movement unfolded into the 1840s, coupled with industrialization and the exponential population growth, the idea of written examinations came to the forefront of the thinking of Horace Mann, the then Secretary of the State Board of Education in Massachusetts (U.S. Congress, Office of Technology Assessment 1992).

Viewing "standardized" testing as a way to ascertain whether students were learning, Mann saw tests as a way to efficiently determine the progress of a growing student population. The idea of standardized tests at that time did not imply norm-referenced types of exams, but rather it was more focused on efficiency and consistency as to how the tests were administered and graded (U.S. Congress, Office of Technology Assessment, 1992). Yet, as Sacks (1999) points out, from the onset when standardized types of tests were first used during Mann's day to the current day of "high-stakes" testing, it has been a process riddled with blatant educational and political misuse.

For example, in early Massachusetts, the tests were intended to ascertain individual student achievement, which was also limited in scope as well, being that the test was comprised of thirty questions that were presumably to cover the entire curriculum for a school year. Not only was there a limitation of questions, but they were often not clear, setting students up for failure and ultimately painting school headmasters in a bad light for a variety of political motives. Finally, despite the intent of those first tests to assess individual student achievement levels, "it turns out, the availability of standardized test results compelled public officials to numerically compare and rank schools . . . This pattern of using such tests for political ends would become all too familiar in the history of American education" (Sacks 1999, 71).

ARRIVAL OF INTELLIGENCE TESTING

In the mid-1800s, Francis Galton, a British psychologist who was deeply influenced by Charles Darwin, forwarded the idea of a statistical method that moved toward a mechanism to measure intelligence quotient as one that is genetically influenced. Galton was indeed an early pioneer of eugenics, a science or philosophy that examines the way people can be improved through controlled genetic selection. With Galton's work, we see a singular narration that merges eugenics, mental measurement, and meritocracy (Sacks 1999).[3]

Later at the dawn of the 1900s, Charles Spearman, another British psychologist and one who admired Galton's work, explored the notion of a two-factor theory of intelligence, arguing a general factor in intelligence known as "g," and based on correlation analysis making connections to specific factors of intelligence called "s." Meanwhile during this same era, James McKeen Cattrell, an American psychologist, conceived the term "mental test" in order to rank differences in intelligence based on the speed at which one sensorially reacts to stimuli (Lagemann 2000; Sacks 1999; U.S. Congress, Office of Technology Assessment 1992; Bertrand and Cebula 1980).

While Galton's and Spearman's work was riddled with problematic assumptions, methodologies, and participant size, and while Cattrell's work was considerably flawed, collectively their work continued the conversation regarding the measuring of intelligence (Lagemann 2000; Sacks 1999).

Rejecting the idea that intelligence is fixed, as Galton suggested, Alfred Binet, a French psychologist during the early 1900s, along with his collaborator Theodore Simon, finally developed an intelligence test.

While Binet and Simon were primarily focused on language and verbal skills, they were not exactly precise in what they were measuring in what became known as the Binet-Simon scale, the original test that served as a model for the later designed IQ test (Janesick 2001; Sacks 1999).

Moreover, while the Binet-Simon scale was lacking when taking into account cultural context and other background influences that one brings to the test, Binet and his colleagues, nevertheless, made clear their test was simply to be used as a diagnostic tool "for assessing the developmental progress of children, and he [Binet] refrained from interpreting the scores on the examinations as the result of some fixed and unchangeable quantity of mental ability endowed at birth" (Sacks 1999, 25). In short, despite Binet suggesting his diagnostic tool be used with caution, when the Binet-Simon scale found its way to the United States, Lewis M. Terman saw the instrument as a pathway to link intelligence with heredity.[4]

In 1916, Terman, a psychologist at Stanford, modified the Binet-Simon scale, which became known as the Stanford-Binet standardized test to measure intelligence; hence, it was during this time that a new term officially came on the scene: intelligence quotient (IQ). Indeed, Terman not only saw IQ tests as supporting a hereditarian viewpoint and placed a high-stakes importance on these tests, he also saw them as useful to compare scores among those taking them, determining categories of individuals based on intelligence.[5] Later, Terman was instrumental in developing the Stanford Achievement Test (SAT) (Lagemann 2000; Sacks 1999; Bertrand and Cebula 1980).

Like the flaws in the Binet-Simon scale, Terman—calling the public-school system the great equalizer—dismissed, therefore, any relevance of one's cultural, economic, home, and social background to how one performed on a test. Yet, despite the latter, in response to the large numbers of recruits that aimed to join the Army during World War I, the Stanford-Binet Scale was widely used to sort out the recruits by rank and jobs.[6] And still later, based on how these tests were used to screen recruits entering the service and the addition of further research on testing, schools embraced these tests. This, then, launched the testing movement as we now know it (Lagemann 2000; Sacks 1999).

In the interest of efficiency and control of information through the guise of the "science" of education, testing became a powerful mechanism in early American education, which takes us back to Thorndike and Dewey. Indeed, while Thorndike (1918) worked on developing standardized tests in the various school disciplines, famously arguing that "whatever exists at all exists in some amount" (16), Dewey was displeased that the testers and quantifiers had won (U.S. Congress, Office of Technology Assessment 1992).

Considered the first standardized achievement test popularly used in the schools, Thorndike created the *Thorndike Handwriting Scale* in 1909, later to be followed with other achievement and aptitude tests (Perrone 1991). Yet, while the quantifiers largely controlled the narrative and standardized testing use was in play, these tests did not dominate the educational landscape in such a way as they do in the current day, which will be explored in the next chapter.

NOTES

1. It is worthwhile to remark that Thorndike never taught children and, as Lagemann (2000) notes, he thought himself more as a psychologist than an educator. The long-term implication of the latter suggests the fostering of a model that asserts that one who is immersed as an educational researcher is one who searches for truth, and one who is a practitioner is who one who simply focuses on application. Furthermore, while Thorndike saw women in particular aptly filling their role as teachers, he viewed teaching as more of a functionary or technical endeavor, and thought men as more gifted for administrative positions and leadership roles. To that end, Thorndike thought "teachers should come to understand their subordinate place in the educational hierarchy" (Lagemann 2000, 60). Presently, while it is true that women populate leadership roles of all types in education, there continues to be a struggle in which teachers continuously negotiate their place in hierarchal systems (see chapter 25).

2. While it is arguable as to when the administering of a grading system exactly came on the scene in U.S. education, it does, however, appear to be clear that grades were not given to students prior to the late 1700s, meaning student feedback was provided with narrative remarks. In 1870, Yale University began using a four-point scale, which then started the path toward grade point average scales, and later to letter grade scales (Marzano 2000).

3. On this point, Sacks (1999) makes an interesting observation regarding Galton by suggesting, "this member of the British aristocracy might, indeed, be considered the father of modern views of meritocracy, in which one succeeds (or not) on the basis of intelligence and wit rather than one's inheritance. Society's role, therefore, was to promote policies and methods that would provide enlightened assistance to nature for selecting the best and brightest for society's most important roles" (19). Clearly, Sacks's observations suggest educational implications in which a confluence of concepts related to economics, opportunity, justice, and the common good collide.

4. Whereas Binet was commissioned by the French government to search for a dependable means to identify children that were mentally "defective" in order to justify their exclusion from regular-education classrooms, Terman's motive was not only to identify "defectives" in order that society can keep them under surveillance, but also to promote the idea that intelligence can be indisputably measured (Sacks 1999).

5. Perrone (1991), however, points out that while IQ tests have been readily used in the schools as a means to categorize, label, and stratify children, they are highly controversial and their use over the years has been curtailed for a variety of reasons, including the reason that "such testing serves *no* educational purpose" (142).

6. Known as the Alpha and Beta tests, these controversial Army intelligence tests determined who would be relegated to the battlefield and who to officer training school. After the war, these tests were modeled as a way to construct new measurement tests for education (Solley 2007; U.S. Congress, Office of Technology Assessment 1992).

TWENTY-TWO
Moving into an Era of High-Stakes Testing

> *Demanding high scores fits nicely with the use of political slogans like "tougher standards" or "accountability" or "raising the bar" . . . The fact is that they usually don't assess the skills and dispositions that matter most.*
>
> (Kohn 2000, 3–7)

Moving forward into the twentieth century, alongside with standardized tests in general use, teacher-made tests were certainly viewed with value, and an increased interest in the arts came to the forefront (Janesick, 2001).[1] It is also notable to point out here that in 1949, Ralph Tyler's *Basic Principles of Curriculum and Instruction* was released, highly influencing the direction of education up to this day.[2]

Now in its thirty-sixth printing, the text asks four central questions (Tyler 1949, 1):

1. What educational purposes should the school seek to attain?
2. What educational experiences can be provided that are likely to attain these purposes?
3. How can these educational experiences be effectively organized?
4. How can we determine whether these purposes are being attained?

It was fundamentally from these questions that the emergence of the categorization of goals, objectives, lesson plans, scope and sequence guides, and mastery of learning evaluations came to be, prompting Slattery (1995) to argue that curriculum development in the United States (and elsewhere) has been significantly influenced by what is characterized as the Tylerian rationale—a rationale, however, that has not gone on without a counter response (see appendix B). Tyler is considered to be the "father" of behavioral objectives by many, and his thought continues to be ever-present in the contemporary educational landscape.

With the launch of Sputnik by the Soviet Union in 1957, an emphasis on science and mathematics education was underscored, with standardized tests as a critical assessment tool. The Vietnam conflict, the Civil Rights Movement, gay rights, children's rights, and Watergate all profoundly became a part of the national conversation in the 1960s and 1970s, impacting the idea of contextually teaching for understanding. While standardized tests were still used for defined reasons, teacher-made tests were still used relative to the curriculum (Janesick 2001).

Yet, still during that era, a restlessness and concern regarding the schools, teachers, what students were learning, their preparation to compete internationally, and how monies were being spent was increasing. Moreover, with the passing of the 1965 Elementary and Secondary Act (ESEA), an arm of President Lyndon Johnson's war on poverty, federal money was allocated for those states in great need in order to assist student learning. The condition, however, was that those programs needed to be evaluated largely through standardized tests, albeit the tests that were being used—modeled on the earlier used Army tests—were of little value (Solley 2007).

With the 1983 *A Nation at Risk* report released under the Reagan administration, a defined shift in how public education and teachers were viewed began to take place. The report declared that test scores were declining, the curriculum was outdated, and the quality of teaching had gone down, all of which contributed to the "rising tide of mediocrity," greatly placing the economic and national security of the nation at risk (United States National Commission on Excellence in Education 1983).[3]

Improving the curriculum in the schools, working on strengthening teacher-education programs, and the adoption of more rigorous measurable standards for both K–12 and university programs was in order. To be sure, the interpretation of what contemporary school reform ought to be about has its most recent foundation dated to *A Nation at Risk*, which influenced the direction of subsequent reform initiatives such as *America 2000* (Bush I), *Goals 2000* (Clinton), *No Child Left Behind Act* (NCLB) (Bush II), and now the *Race to the Top* program (Obama). As one studies each of these reform packages, it becomes apparent that the emphasis on assessment increasingly rises in importance. And with NCLB, the culmination of that importance takes center stage.[4]

A HIGH-STAKES WORLD AND ACCOUNTABILITY

No longer simply labeled as testing, but now referred to as "high-stakes" testing, our present conversations of what is critical in school reform has mutated into what can be characterized as corporate speak. In other words, we have become so enamored with the convenience of explaining school reform with detached terminology such as outcomes, results, performance, monetary rewards, takeover, competition, and comparing and contrasting that we have created a system that is analogous to describing a for-profit corporation, which ultimately results in the creation of "winners" and "losers."

Consequently, in order to determine the accuracy of who the winners and losers are, we have to clamp down in securing the tool that protects that interest. In the end, this type of system fosters the objectification of school-aged children, possesses an extraordinarily constricted view of what is educationally important, and largely blames teachers for anything that ails education. Indeed, while Theodore Thorndike's influence won over John Dewey in the early twentieth century, it also has culminated into a present-day toxic environment in which school-aged youngsters have joined Dewey in defeat (see previous chapter).[5]

For some perspective, whereas in 1950 those who completed high school took only approximately three standardized tests through their entire K–12 experience, not to mention that the results of the tests were not emphasized and certainly were not headlines in the local media, those in 1991 who completed high school took an average of eighteen to twenty-one standardized tests, with most being administered in the K–5 grades, certainly with results being a critical subject of conversation in the home, school, community, and the media (Perrone 1991).

Fast forward to the current day and, according to a report by Bowman (2014), students on average will take more than sixty standardized tests during their K–12 schooling experience, which does not take into account noncompulsory tests such as ACT or the SAT.[6] Costing the states 1.7 billion annually in the name of accountability and what is known as data-driven instruction, "standardized testing has swelled and mutated, like a creature in one of those old horror movies, to the point that it now threatens to swallow our schools whole" (Kohn 2000, 1).

Indeed, accountability and reform are topics at the forefront of the modern-day education landscape, dominating the discourse at state department of education gatherings, local school board meetings, at school-site faculty meetings, and at family dinner tables. In short, the sum of the discussions has so predominantly linked the notion of accountability and school reform to such concepts as high-stakes testing, achievement, performance, and results that one online dictionary definition of accountability now has an exclusive definition just for education. That is, accountability is defined as "a policy of holding schools and teachers accountable for students' academic progress by linking such progress with funding, for salaries, maintenance, etc."[7]

In a nutshell, school reform therefore unfolds as teachers are held accountable for assuring that students do well on high-stakes tests. The assumption is that when the students *perform* well on such tests, reform is taking place, teacher accountability is working, and schools are both eligible and deserving of monetary rewards. It is nothing short of disturbing that two complex, yet extraordinary concepts such as accountability and reform have been reduced to extremely narrow terms, particularly in a world of education where manifestations of human complexity are a natural common occurrence, paradox an ongoing conundrum, and life-giving engaged pedagogy a continuous challenge (Kirylo and Nauman 2006).

This reductionist explanation of what contemporary education has become did not come overnight; indeed it has been in the making for over a century, notably heightened in the last forty years, beginning with *A Nation at Risk* to the present day. In fact, with the rhetoric declared by eager politicians vying for a vote and furthered by the media working to get a story, the notion of education reform can be characterized as what Kirylo and Nauman (2006) call the institutionalization of the depersonalization of education, resulting in an extraordinary climatic shift on how human beings are being regulated in a school setting (Slattery and Rapp 2003).[8]

Regarding her son's achievement on a standardized test, a parent in Boise, Idaho, put it this way: "Teachers were mesmerized by the numbers . . . They were in awe of him. Because he did so well on the test, in a way they didn't see *him*. They saw him as his test scores" (Sacks 1999, 65). And there you have it. School-aged youngsters lose with a system of accountability that turns them into a number or a score. To state another way, as Kohn (2010) suggests, we have turned children into data. This "data-driven" phenomenon through an overemphasis on standardized tests has clearly been harmful.

NOTES

1. As a matter of fact, standardized tests were sparingly used in the lower grades prior to 1965. It was not until the late 1970s, with many placing aside our understandings of how children develop, that testing filtered to the primary grades, which is now common practice (Perrone 1991).

2. Tyler was a significant contributor to the designing of the National Assessment of Educational Progress (NAEP). First administered in 1969, NAEP are norm-referenced tests given every two years across the country. Sometimes referred to as the Nation's Report Card, a sampling representative of students in fourth, eighth, and twelfth grades takes these tests, which are generally focused on reading, math, science, and writing. Designed to track collective achievement growth over time in states, individual scores are not made public.

3. *A Nation at Risk* was clearly a highly charged document, largely placing the presumed failure of education at the feet of educators and public education, which provided political fuel for politicians to push an agenda that has morphed into what is now characterized as the corporatization or marketization of education. In fact, it is noteworthy to point out that in their revealing book, *The Manufactured Crises* (1995), the authors David Berliner and Bruce Biddle make a compelling argument, challenging the data that drove the publication of *A Nation at Risk* report, asserting the quality

of schools are not failing as purported by the report. Moreover, Berliner and Biddle not only provide insightful suggestions, but also suggest that the larger problems confronting schools are economic and social, including poverty.

4. While Clinton's Goals 2000: Educate America Act *recommended* testing for grades 4, 8, and 12 to ascertain whether standards were being realized, in W. Bush's NCLB Act, testing was *mandatory* in those grades. The stakes were certainly higher under NCLB, tied to "grade retention, admittance into special programs, graduation, admission into college, and whether or not schools remain open and teachers get to keep their jobs" (Solley 2007, 33).

5. Thorndike obviously contributed to the standardized testing movement as we know it today, but as Perrone (1977) makes clear, it is important to point out that while one may argue the assumptions that guided Thorndike's thinking about education and learning, he was a thoughtful researcher on forwarding quality measurement instruments, which led the trending away from the largely distasteful eugenic thinking that guided the work of Terman and others (see previous chapter).

6. As a note of distinction among various types of standardized tests that can be administered, there are achievement tests (testing what one knows as a result of instruction), which can come in the form of norm-referenced tests (generally tests that can be administered nationally, in which scores can be compared and ranked) or criterion reference tests (generally state types of tests in which attained scores are based on meeting the criteria or standard). Aptitude tests are those that assess one's capability or suitability for something (e.g., ACT, SAT, GRE), and psychological tests come in a variety of forms (e.g., I.Q., personality, attitude, interest tests).

7. See http://www.factmonster.com/ipd/A0305025.html.

8. Hancock (2005) argues that members of the newspaper media specifically, particularly those who conduct school reporting, should become more intimately informed regarding the complexities of schooling. Being more informed would greatly assist them in probing more deeply, asking more reflectively, and reporting more carefully regarding the happenings in school systems and in individual schools.

TWENTY-THREE
Four Harmful Effects of High-Stakes Testing

> *In recent years, there's a strong tendency to require assessment of children and teachers so that you have to teach to tests. And the test determines what happens to the child and what happens to the teacher. That's guaranteed to destroy any meaningful educational process.*
>
> (Chomsky 2015)

Major educational organizations, such as the American Educational Research Association (AERA), National Association for the Education of Young Children (NAEYC), International Reading Association (IRA), National Council of Teachers of English (NCTE), American Evaluation Association (AEA), Association of Childhood Education International (ACEI), National Parent Teacher Association (PTA), and the American Psychological Association (APA) have either written position statements or resolutions regarding the overuse of standardized tests.

Moreover, a diverse range of notable scholars such as Linda-Darling Hammond, Diane Ravitch, Alfie Kohn, Peter Sacks, Donaldo Macedo, Deborah Meier, and Theodore Sizer have urged caution in how standardized tests are used. Finally, a growing contingency of teachers and parents has been gaining momentum in "opting out" and simply—but strongly—saying "no" to standardized tests.

Yet despite the resistance from a variety of exceptional corners, the overuse of standardized tests nevertheless has blindly been the bugle call for politicians and policy makers, infecting the educational landscape, hurting school-aged youngsters, and terribly shaping public opinion.

With the advent of the Common Core State Standards (CCSS), the emphasis on standardized tests clearly remains at the forefront of the educational picture.[1] Take, for example, a 2014 newspaper report written by Diane C. Lore (2014) in Staten Island, New York, when she began her story with the following:

> "Ok, this came home Friday. Ugh and its only October!" said South Shore mom Desiree Oddo-Hardison. She was referring to a letter from Totten Intermediate School asking her to send in $30 to purchase "Common Core Coach"—a set of four workbooks—two in math and two in language arts—for her son's teacher to use in class to prepare students to take state standardized tests in the spring. "Common Core is a huge problem, with way to [sic] much emphasis on testing, as this letter clearly states," Ms. Oddo-Hardison said, taking to Facebook to vent her frustration.

Nevertheless, at this writing, the CCSS have been adopted by forty-three states, purporting to be high-quality standards in the areas of language arts and mathematics in order to provide high-school students with the knowledge and skills to enable them to be prepared for college, career, and even life, irrespective of wherever one decides to reside.[2]

Under the umbrella of the Obama administration's Race to the Top Program, with the dangling of federal dollars to entice school systems all over the country, monies were awarded to states who agreed to adopt the CCSS, which are linked to a high-stakes standardized testing system called Partnership for Assessment of Readiness for College and Careers (PARCC) and Smarter Balanced Assessment Consortium (SBAC), all linked to big business, namely Pearson Publishing Company.

Cash-strapped state systems all over the country were hardly resistant to the conditions that came with adopting CCSS and its emphasis on testing. Albert Einstein is credited with stating that insanity is doing the same thing over and over again and expecting different results. Perhaps that quotation is timeworn, but there is no other way of putting it regarding the trajectory education has been on, particularly for the last four decades.

Indeed, testing is swallowing our schools. And that is insane; we are spinning our wheels to nowhere, but continue to think we are going somewhere, expecting something different with our overuse of standardized testing. Darling-Hammond (1997) rightly argues that "bureaucratic solutions to problems of practice will always fail because effective teaching is not routine, students are not passive, and questions of practice are not simple, predictable, or standardized" (67). In short, this perpetual road of standardized testing has led us on an educational dark path in four fundamental ways.

1. Narrows the Curriculum

First, the emphasis on testing has extraordinarily narrowed the curriculum, coercing teachers to simply focus on prescribed areas of certain disciplines that will be tested. As a consequence, the arts in all its forms have greatly been deprived; social studies and the sciences have received less attention; and especially for the very young, the idea of play and recess has been dismissed as frivolous. Moreover, a climate of testing is creating a teaching and learning environment of fear, in which students and teachers resist taking risks and exploring deeper on a respective theme for fear of deviating from the set curriculum (Solley 2007).

And those who are affected the most with this narrowing of the curriculum are largely poor and minority students, who are reduced to minimal options and opportunities in order to be drilled and skilled to prepare for testing, all in an effort to "measure" their "growth."

Regarding that phenomenon, Kozol (2005) explains it this way:

> As damaging as the obsessive emphasis on testing often proves to be for kids in general, I believe that the effects are still more harmful in those schools in which the resources available to help the children learn the skills that will be measured by these tests are fewest, the scores they get are predictably the lowest, and the strategies resorted to by the principals in order to escape the odium attaching to a disappointing set of numbers tend to be the most severe. (110)

To be sure, this entire effort has led to the dumbing down of the curriculum, dulling the entire schooling experience (Solley 2007; Sacks 1999).

Driven by the thinking of the NCLB Act, and now the Race to the Top Program, is the mistaken notion that the ability to measure schools is equated with fixing them (Darling-Hammond 2004).[3] As Rose (1989) asserts:

> We are a nation obsessed with evaluating our children, with calibrating their exact distance from some ideal benchmark. In the name of excellence, we test and measure them—as individuals, as a group—and we rejoice or despair over the results. The sad thing is that though we strain to see, we miss so much. All students cringe under the scrutiny, but those most harshly affected, least successful in the competition, possess some of our greatest unperceived riches. (xi)

2. Creates a Stressful Environment

Second, an emphasis on high-stakes testing has created a schooling environment that has cultivated stress and pressure, not only negatively impacting the lives of teachers and administrators, but naturally those of children. With respect to the latter, children are led on a path of confusion.

On the one hand, teachers routinely advise students to work carefully, take their time to think through their work, and to focus on critical thinking, but when it comes to standardized assessment instruments, all of the latter becomes artificial musings when students are forced to respond within a prescribed standardized test time. Moreover, a results-orientated climate clearly undermines process, which not only creates havoc on a forming self-concept, but also causes great confusion in forming that self-concept (Solley 2007; Perrone 1991).

Cizek and Burg (2006) argue that the notion of test anxiety is not a new happening, but in times past, the manifestation of that anxiety in a school setting was collectively a mild response to taking tests of any kind. However, in an era of high-stakes testing, the appearance of anxiety has not only notably risen, but is also acutely experienced with younger and younger children. Test anxiety naturally creates a stressful schooling environment, which is manifested in students in a variety of ways. For example, see appendix C and consider table 23.1.

In addition, a high-stakes testing environment has had a remarkable anxiety-inducing effect on teachers as well, receiving pressure from administrators and parents, not only adversely affecting teacher morale, but, as earlier mentioned, simply reducing them to teach to the test (Cizek and Burg 2006). In short, for teachers, our preoccupation with testing "is one of the most demoralizing, energy-draining forces in education today" (Graves 2001, 80).

Table 23.1. General Effects of Test Anxiety on Students

Effect	Relationship(s)
Stress	Test anxiety can induce symptoms of stress, such as crying, acting out, verbalizations
Attitude toward tests and testing	Test anxiety can diminish effort or increase student apathy toward testing
Attitude toward self	Test anxiety can reinforce, induce poor self-esteem or poor/inaccurate self-evaluation ("I can't do anything," "I am so stupid")
Test behavior	Test anxiety can prompt cheating (e.g., sharing or copying of answers obtaining/using illegal copies of "secure" materials)
Academic motivation	Test anxiety can decrease student motivation to learn in general
Motivation (future)	Test anxiety can be associated with dropping out of school, grade retention, graduation, placement in special programs/classes
Test anxiety	Effects of test anxiety can "cycle back" to result in successive poor test performance, leading to increased levels of test anxiety

Source: Cizek and Burg 2006, 31.

3. Dulls Motivation and Ignores Appropriate Practice

Third, with a focus on "results" and "scores" or extrinsic measures, the consequence of such focus dulls intrinsic motivation to learn, not to mention the joy of learning in itself is greatly reduced. Clearly, an environment of testing has resulted in an approach that focuses on low-level skills in order to assure the possibilities toward working to mark the best answer (Solley 2007; Sacks 1999).

There is scant evidence in which the overuse of standardized testing has substantively improved learning; in fact, learning has been greatly reduced in such a way that developmentally appropriate practices have been largely ignored, yielding, as earlier mentioned, to skilling and drilling, particularly affecting those young people who have been historically disenfranchised. What obviously gets lost are children and their excitement about learning and their natural curiosity to discover and inquire.

Particularly for primary-level children, these tests are extraordinarily inappropriate. As Perrone (1991) puts it: "These are years when children's growth is most uneven, in large measure idiosyncratic; the skills needed for success in school are in their most fluid acquisitional stages. Implications of failure in these years can be especially devastating" (133). Indeed, these tests from very early on have subjected youngsters to unnecessary labels, determining whether they get accepted in certain programs, whether they should pass a grade or not, whether they are "slow" or not, and a host of other labels that not only harm children, but also have no substantive educational benefit (Perrone 1991).

As if that were not enough, teacher professionalism in making judgments and decisions has been undermined by this entire process, all of which has forced them to teach in such a way that counters what they know that best addresses the needs of their diverse student population (Solley 2007).

4. Promotes Teacher Turnover and Is Cost-Prohibitive

Fourth, testing has resulted in many excellent teachers exiting the profession not only because they are more and more viewed as simple functionaries subjected to overcrowded classrooms without support, but also—to reiterate—our fanatical focus on tests, scores, and results has created an enormously stressful working environment.

The median teacher turnover rate is 17 percent nationally, but that rate jumps to 20 percent in urban settings. Within three years into the profession, it is estimated a third of new teachers leave, and after five years, approximately 46 percent of them are gone. With respect to recruiting, hiring, and attempts to hold onto new teachers, this "revolving door" has translated into an estimated annual cost of $7 billion (Kopkowski 2008).

Finally, schooling that is focused on an unhealthy competitive environment that is more interested in comparing and contrasting numbers, ratings, and scores instead of the welfare of human beings has not only shortchanged precious instructional time, but also has come with a monumental price tag. For example, based on a recent American Federation of Teachers (AFT) study examining a midsized undisclosed school district in the Midwest and one in the East, the cost and instructional time spent on standardized testing has increased from NCLB to the Race to the Top program.

The breakdown per annual pupil spending in the Midwestern district was as follows: grades K–2 (approximately $200); grades 3–8 ($600 or more); and grades 9–11 ($400–600), and the breakdown per annual pupil spending in the Eastern school district was as follows: grades 1–2 (approximately $400); grades 3–5 (between $700-$800); and grades 6–11 (more than $1,100).

In addition, the report stated that one district not only administered fourteen different assessments annually to all students in at least one grade level, but also other assessments were administered at various times during the year in other subjects, tallying to thirty-four different times tests were annually administered. And the other district administered twelve different assessments that comprised of forty-seven different times they were annually administered.

The report also stated that on average, test preparation in the targeted testing grades can annually take anywhere from sixty to more than 110 hours. To put another way, with testing preparation and testing days combined, one district used nineteen full school days, and in the targeted testing grades in the other district, a month and a half was used. Lastly, while in one school district if testing were discarded, twenty to forty minutes of instruction time in most grades could be added to the school day, the other district could add nearly a whole class period to the school day (Nelson 2013; Strauss 2013).

To be sure, this AFT report is simply indicative of the tip of the iceberg regarding the time and cost given to standardized testing all over the country; consider NCLB, which emerged in 2002—the price tag of annual standardized test went from $423 million to approximately $1.1 billion in 2008 to $1.7 billion in 2014.

A MORATORIUM IS IN ORDER

To encapsulate, when it comes to the overuse of standardized tests, they have not only harmed the quality of teaching and have chased good teachers away, but they also have had very little impact on improving learning. Moreover, considering the political nature in which they have been used, the way they have damaged the teaching and learning process, the costs of them, and the havoc they have played in the lives of school-aged youth and their families, it is no wonder that numerous professional organizations, educators, and parents have called for a moratorium on a system of assessment that has gone wild, has gone rogue, has gotten incredibly out of control.[4]

With the ultimate goal of assessment as a process to improve teaching and learning, the question, therefore, if our perverted use of standardized testing is not fitting the bill, what is a more constructive direction that should necessarily be considered in order to positively impact teaching and learning? Two closely associated processes to emphasize, which are examined in the next chapter, are (1) to realize the practical, qualitative, and holistic value of what it means to formatively assess, and (2) to feature an assessment approach that is portfolio orientated.

NOTES

1. Emerging on the scene in 2009, CCSS came about in response to an apparent inconsistency from state to state as to what students are to learn in each grade level across the country, and a purported inertia of student progress and the diminishment of them being able to compete internationally. Therefore in the name of continuity, progress, and competitiveness, CCSS were designed and created under the canopy of the Council of Chief State School Officers (CCSSO) and the National Governors Association Center for Best Practices (NGA Center). Though claimed to not be a prescribed curriculum or to be a vehicle to undermine states' education rights, having very well-defined standards that are aimed to particularly foster a deeper level of thinking will presumably inform teachers what is to be covered in actual classroom practice.

2. See http://www.corestandards.org/about-the-standards/.

3. The assumption is that if something can be measured, data then can be provided in order to evaluate, assisting in the making of concrete decisions. In the case of NCLB and the Race to the Top Program, the decisions that are made based on the evaluation of that data if certain criteria or scores are not met as well as the impact on students, teachers, and schools are quite punitive. Whether a low standardized score forces a student to repeat a grade; or students don't collectively show "growth" in a particular class, declaring the teacher ineffective; or whether low test scores label a school a D or F, placing it at risk of closure—all of these ways of measuring are presumably going to have an impact on motivating students, teachers, and schools to improve. While perhaps in few instances the labeling and shaming may lead to change, "a better approach would be to invest in the needed improvements in such schools in the first place, and to measure their progress on a variety of indicators in ways that give the schools credit for improvements they produce for the students they serve" (Darling-Hammond 2004, 14–15).

4. For example, see http://dianeravitch.net/2014/11/25/fairtest-demand-to-limit-testing-escalates/.

TWENTY-FOUR
Emphasizing Formative and Portfolio Assessments

> *Where assessment is educative, we hear classroom and hallway conversations that are different than those heard in schools that use traditional assessment methods. Students are no longer asking teachers, "Is this what you want?" or "Is this going to be on the test?"*
>
> (Wiggins 1998, 1)

Assessment is not something a teacher does *to* a student, but rather is an activity that a teacher does *with* and *for* a student, suggesting, as was pointed out in chapter 20, that the notion of assessment is quite different from the idea of testing (Wiggins 1993).

That is, to also reiterate, the notion of being an assessor not only assumes one possesses a deep understanding of why s/he assesses, when s/he assesses, and how s/he assesses in order to impact student learning in constructive ways, but also assumes the stance is one that is viewed through a lens of inquiry, collaboratively works with students, and depends on varying forms of assessments in order to make adjustments as needed to maximize the teaching and learning process (NCTE 2013). In that light, therefore, a central way to move toward that end is to consider the important place of formative assessments and portfolio assessments.

FORMATIVE ASSESSMENTS

Formative assessments are key to the everydayness of the teaching and learning process in order that teachers can appropriately gauge student progress. It is a process that leads teachers through a continuous deeper understanding of how they pedagogically connect to their students in order to better realize how and what they are learning.

And while formative assessment is a dynamic that involves process, occurs during instruction, provides feedback to teachers and students, and assists in making instructional and learning adjustments, Popham (2008) asserts that there are multiple ways to explain formative assessments and that there is no single "official" definition of the concept. Hence, he offers what is a useful, succinct definition: "Formative assessment is a planned process in which assessment-elicited evidence of students' status is used by teachers to adjust their ongoing instructional procedures or by students to adjust their current learning tactics" (6).

As a way to more concretely illuminate the latter, take for example the athletic trainer or a music teacher, mentoring, watching, or examining the mentee in his/her every move. This examination allows for the trainer or music teacher to collaboratively work with the mentee, which then allows for an exchange in communication to occur, meaningfully guiding the teaching and learning process in a constructive way.[1]

As is with the case of formative assessment in general, formative assessment is a planned process, not a test, but one that involves a variety of activities that engages students and teachers in the teaching and learning process (Popham 2008).

The National Council of Teachers of English (NCTE 2013) makes clear the positive impact that formative assessment has on student learning, recognizing that its process is clear about the specificity of its goals, the educative value of its goals, is aware of student background knowledge and skills, recognizes the steps involved in attaining goals, and necessitates student responsibility in his/her learning and in reaching desired goals.

Within that continuous process, teachers are involved in such a way to provide feedback through a variety of means, such as conversations, interviews, conferences, rubrics, checklists, and grades. Table 24.1 provides a helpful picture of what formative assessment is and what it is not.

As the table reveals, the propeller that drives formative assessment is feedback, suggesting it is an ongoing constructive process in which the student is able to refine, redo, or modify that which is being formatively assessed.

For example, the student who is busily working on a paper and seeks the teacher's feedback regarding the paper's direction, flow, and theme is then able to use that feedback in continuing on with the paper. In other words, an assessment is "only *formative* if it recurs as a task in which I can learn from feedback to improve at the 'same' task" (Wiggins 2011). Ultimately, however, when the paper is turned in at the deadline for a final grade, the assessment process then becomes one that is summative "if it is the final chance, the 'summing up' of student performance" (Wiggins 2011).[2]

Wiggins (2012) goes on to mention that providing feedback is driven by the assumption that one is mindful of the ultimate goal, which then

Table 24.1. What Is and Is Not a Formal Assessment

Formative Assessments DO:	Formative Assessments DO NOT:
Highlight the needs of each student	View all students as being, or needing to be, at the same place in their learning
Provide immediately useful feedback to students and teachers	Provide feedback weeks or months later
Occur as a planned and intentional part of the learning in a classroom	Always occur at the same time for each student
Focus on progress or growth	Focus solely on a number, score, or level
Support goal setting within the classroom curriculum	Occur outside of authentic learning experiences
Answer questions the teacher has about students' learning	Have parameters that limit teacher involvement
Reflect the goals and intentions of the teachers and the students	Look like mini-versions of predetermined summative assessments
Rely on teacher expertise and interpretation	Rely on outsiders to score and analyze results
Occur in the context of classroom life	Interrupt or intrude upon classroom life
Focus on responsibility and care	Focus on accountability
Inform immediate next steps	Focus on external mandates
Consider multiple kinds of information, based in a variety of tools or strategies	Focus on a single piece of information
Allow teachers and students to better understand the learning process in general and the learning process for these students in particular	Exclude teachers and students from assessing through the whole learning process

Source: NCTE 2013, 6.

drives the purpose of the feedback. Therefore, Wiggins continues, feedback is goal referenced (i.e., goal-related information is provided); is tangible and transparent (i.e., however it is communicated, feedback is clearly understood); is actionable (i.e., feedback is specific, concrete, and useful, which leads to action); is user-friendly (i.e., feedback is easily understood, and not riddled with technical language and information overload); is timely (i.e., feedback is provided in a timely fashion based on the need as opposed to feedback that is delayed); is ongoing (i.e., ongoing feedback in "real time" monumentally impacts the final product); and is consistent (i.e., feedback is trustworthy, accurate, and stable, and teachers and students are on the same page regarding expectations). In the end, as Popham (2008) states, "FORMATIVE ASSESSMENT WORKS!" (1).

PORTFOLIO ASSESSMENTS

Portfolios are a collection of student work that is purposely selected over a period of time. And depending on their purpose, portfolios can be varied in their arrangement, yet with a sense of authenticity that undergirds that arrangement. That is, authentic assessments are those that reflect the work of students that were thoughtfully produced through meaningful activities and projects (Mueller 2014).

Within that process, students are engaged in reflection, self-assessment, and goal setting, a metacognitive endeavor that naturally includes a focus on effort, improvement, and progress. This endeavor positively impacts learning in such a way that it is not qualitatively captured in a focus that simply concentrates on grades, scores, and final product (Mueller 2014).

Describing authentic assessment as an integrated, varied, and ongoing process that occurs within instructional practice, Player (2000) further explains:

> This process is always contextualized and connected to a student's experiences. It promotes communication and learning by encouraging students to actively construct their own understanding. Furthermore, it aims to support, rather than simply measure, learning. Authentic assessment may take many different forms, such as: portfolios of a student's work, investigations, experiments, group projects, and oral presentations. Including a variety of forms, authentic assessment ensures that all students are given an opportunity to show what they can do, and teachers have the information needed to construct a balanced and true assessment of each student. Authentic assessment enhances the learning experience because students and teachers construct their own understanding from their classroom experiences and then check their understanding against their own views, the views of others, their observations, and their reflections.

While a foundational feature of portfolios is authenticity and while they can be described in multiple ways and can come in a variety of forms, Danielson and Abrutyn (1997) assert that portfolios can come in the form of three major types: working portfolios (works in progress); display, showcase, or best works portfolios (display of best work); and assessment portfolios (documentation of student learning). And while there is a certain amount of interrelatedness among the three forms of portfolios, it is the last one that will be the focus here.

In constructing an assessment portfolio, the content of the curriculum is the focus of what is to be placed in the portfolio. Whether the discipline is mathematics or whether the focus is on persuasive writing in an English class, the artifact(s) (i.e., piece[s] of work) inserted in the portfolio ought to reflect what the student has learned or the mastery of a particular curriculum objective. This process can be designed over a designated period of time or the entire academic year (Danielson and Abrutyn, 1997).

The following provides eight essential steps that go into the process of thoughtfully constructing an assessment portfolio system (Danielson and Abrutyn 1997, 6):

1. Determine the curricular objectives to be addressed through the portfolio.
2. Determine the decisions that will be made based on the portfolio assessments. Will the assessments be used for high-stakes assessment at certain levels of schooling (for example, to enable students to make the transition from middle school to high school)?
3. Design assessment tasks for the curricular objectives. Ensure that the task matches instructional intentions and adequately represents the content and skills (including the appropriate level of difficulty) students are expected to attain. These considerations will ensure the validity of the assessment tasks.
4. Define the criteria for each assessment task and establish performance standards for each criterion.
5. Determine who will evaluate the portfolio entries. Will they be teachers from the students' own school? Teachers from another school? Or does the state identify and train evaluators?
6. Train teachers or other evaluators to score the assessments. This will ensure the reliability of the assessments.
7. Teach the curriculum, administer assessments, collect them in portfolios, score assessments.
8. As determined in Step 2, make decisions based on the assessments in the portfolios.

As opposed to the shortcomings of standardized tests as a "high stakes" summative assessment tool, a portfolio system that is designed with a standard of validity and reliability with well-thought criteria and scoring rubrics can serve as a more holistic representation of student learning and can serve as a powerful summative assessment tool (Solley 2007; Wiggins 1998; Danielson and Abrutyn 1997).

To be sure, the advantages and value of portfolios are numerous, including the fostering of critical thinking and reflection; it involves performance and product; it connects the learner with her/his world and experience; it is flexible, enabling shared responsibility between teacher and student; provides ongoing feedback; and ultimately is an authentic engaging process that unites teacher, student, and families in that process (Mueller 2014; Solley 2007; Janesick 2001; Player 2000).

DEMANDS COMMITMENT TO THE PROCESS

A combination focus on formative assessment and a portfolio assessment system clearly demands a concentrated effort, know how, and commitment by teachers to better ascertain how and what their students are learning, all impacting a more vibrant, holistic, appropriate, and healthy learning environment for students. As we move more and more toward that end, John Dewey will smile.

NOTES

1. To perhaps make even clearer when it comes to elucidating the difference between formative and summative assessment, imagine the athletic trainer/music teacher working with the mentee, and simply relying on a summative approach to assess his/her progress. That process implies that after the trainer/music teacher inculcates the required technique(s), the mentee then needs to demonstrate whether s/he does it correctly. However, the feedback from the mentor won't be given until weeks or months later. Of course, receiving feedback weeks or months later provides very little, if any, instructive value to the mentee who is attempting to learn something related to athletics or music. Yet, it is that very system that is currently used when it comes to standardized testing.

2. There are several purposes for the administering of grades, including for administrative purposes (e.g., matriculation/retention of students, school transfers, university entrance), to provide feedback to students, guidance, instructional planning, and motivation (Marzano 2000). To be sure, the assigning of grades can be a controversial affair and even a practice which some would like to see abandoned; however, whatever value system (grades, portfolios, rubrics, scales, to name a few) that is put into place to judge a student's final product, it must be one that is developmentally appropriate, accurate, fair, and clearly understood.

Section VII

Teacher as Leader: Hierarchy, Poverty, and the Village

Where there is no vision, the people perish.

Proverbs 29:18

TWENTY-FIVE
Teacher as Leader

You don't need a title to be a leader in life.

(Sanborn 2006, xii)

As suggested throughout this text, teachers are those who guide, inculcate, and influence, continuously and reflectively monitoring how they are guiding, what they are inculcating, and what kind of influence they hope to be. The dynamic of this monitoring contextually recognizes that the teacher acts on the following:

- What it means to teach from the inside out;
- The understanding that education is about entering into diverse relationships;
- The realization that a critical goal is to inspire;
- An awareness of the place of educational psychology;
- The knowledge of the five components of knowledge; and
- The recognition of the place and purpose of assessment.

The collective latter, of course, succinctly captures the various themes highlighted in the first six sections of this book, foundationally framing teaching with purpose.

In the final analysis, therefore, because a teacher is one who guides, inculcates, and influences, by definition, a teacher is a leader. As leadership guru John C. Maxwell (n.d.) succinctly puts it, ultimately, "leadership is influence—nothing more, nothing less." That, added to John Dewey's prompting in his writings, education is life itself, and in life for one to lead, as Mark Sanborn intimates in the epigraph, no title is necessary in an endeavor that goes about to influence others.

At the time of the 1996 release of the noteworthy book—with its telling title—*Awakening the Sleeping Giant: Leadership Development for Teachers* by Marilyn Katzenmeyer and Gayle Moller, the notion of teacher leadership was somewhat unexplored territory. Consequently, as the authors rightly suggest in their work "awakening the sleeping giant" was past due with untapped leadership talents, gifts, and insights being relatively underused. Three editions later from that 1996 text and now that a plethora of literature that focuses on teacher leadership is quite apparent, the concept is not so foreign anymore.

And it is true that teachers are taking on more formal leadership roles (e.g., mentorships, instructional leaders, department chairs, literacy coaches, learning facilitators, lead/master teachers, and curriculum specialists) (Katzenmeyer and Moller 2009; Danielson 2007; Harrison and Killion 2007) and informal leadership roles (e.g., organically emerge among their peers, take initiative, and command respect) (Danielson 2007). Yet while the latter is encouraging, we continue to struggle with the notion of teacher leadership in theory and practice, still looking for the "sleeping giant" to more fully awake from its slumber.

FORMAL LEADERSHIP ROLES AND KNOWING YOUR PLACE

Particularly in hierarchal school systems or top-down management school organizational schemes, the connection between "leader" and "teacher" is not a concept that has been historically linked or necessarily even encouraged. At the state level, this type of structure generally moves spirally downward (with some individual state variations) beginning with a state board of education, to a state superintendent of education, to the local school board of education, to the local superintendent, to central office coordinators, to local school principals, and finally to teachers at the school.

In this paradigm, while teachers may be tacitly acknowledged as leaders within their classroom practice, their authority and influence outside the classroom when it comes to policy and state-, system-, and school-wide decisions have been shortchanged, perpetuating a system that maintains the subordinate or dependent nature of the role of the teacher (Murphy 2005).

This kind of system troublingly cultivates an "I am *just* a teacher" attitude among many teachers themselves, and disturbingly fosters a patronizing "You are *just* a teacher" (i.e., know your place) unsaid viewpoint among many in the higher echelon of that hierarchal food chain, all of which works to disempower teachers from being involved, speaking out, or challenging questionable policy decisions.

Indeed, whether it is the questioning of CCSS, standardized testing practices, or a variety of local school decisions that are in disagreement with a teacher or teachers, the problem is those who don't "buy in," not the hierarchal chieftains who make and enforce structural decisions from the top down (e.g., policymakers, school board, superintendents, school administrators). All of this is indicative of minimizing the professionalization of what it means to be a teacher and is reflective of how the teaching profession is viewed by many, clearly obstructing the advancement of teacher leadership.

The issue, therefore, in a hierarchal structure, regardless of how knowledgeable, insightful, and creative individual teachers may be, is that the structure not only places them in a subordinate role, but they may also be characterized as insubordinate, a rebel, or too outspoken when it comes to bringing up concerns or issues relative to the very structure itself, whether it be at the local school, system, or state level.

Moreover, in such hierarchal systems, if individual teachers desire to "move up" into a leadership position, they must move out of the classroom. The implication of such language as "moving up" or actions that necessitate one to move out of the classroom to assume a leadership position suggests that teachers are, in fact, down and must understand their place as underlings.

For many teachers, as Danielson (2007) suggests, this type of infrastructure is unfulfilling and frustrating; Danielson further explains:

> *Teaching is a flat profession.* In most professions, as the practitioner gains experience, he or she has the opportunity to exercise greater responsibility and assume more significant challenges. This is not true of teaching. The 20-year veteran's responsibilities are essentially the same as those of the newly licensed novice. In many settings, the only way for a teacher to extend his or her influence is to become an administrator. Many teachers recognize that this is not the right avenue for them. The job of an administrator entails work that does not interest them, but they still have the urge to exercise wider influence in their schools and in the profession. (14, author's emphasis)

Indeed, therefore, while it is true that the notion of teacher leadership "is an idea whose time has come" (Danielson 2007, 19), we obviously continue to grapple with its meaning, its intent, and what it actually looks like in practice simply because "the term *teacher leadership* conjures different images and meanings for different people" (Fraser 2008, 18). And a significant part of that grappling is being able to authentically make sense of it in light of a hierarchal school system.

Hierarchal systems are enamored with formal titles, no different from when it comes to characterizing teacher leaders. That is, such titles as mentor, curriculum coordinator, lead teacher, instructional coach, department head, and so on formally signify teacher leadership roles, albeit representing arms of the established system (Wasley 1991). The latter point has been more particularly heightened during an era of standardization and so-called accountability, in which increased demands have been placed on school principals, intensifying their reliance on those latter-said, formal teacher leadership roles (Johnson and Donaldson 2007).

Hence, it can be argued that teacher leadership exhibited in this fashion should pose minimal to no threat to the school principal who relishes in holding on to his/her power. To put another way, overextended principals welcome more assistance, which comes in the form of willing teachers who are given "leadership" titles, but generally remain under the principal's thumb.

Clearly, the filling of formal roles by teachers as department heads, instructional coaches, and other related undertakings necessitate leadership abilities, and naturally has its place at a school setting. But, in the end, those and other similar roles largely place yet another bureaucratic layer in a hierarchal system, further emphasizing the message to "know your place."

NO TITLES NECESSARY AND ACTING HORIZONTALLY

On the other hand, teacher leadership from a more informal perspective in which a school principal freely taps into the strengths, gifts, talents, initiatives, and willingness of the teachers in the school greatly depends on how secure a principal is in herself/himself in order to share power. To be sure, this is not an easy happening for many principals (or school systems) who want to hold on to their power, certainly making it true that "not every school is hospitable to the emergence of teacher leaders, particularly informal teacher leaders" (Danielson 2007, 18).

Consequently, whether thoughtful teachers find themselves in either formal teacher leadership roles that may question the hierarchy, or informal leadership roles in which they find themselves bumping against the wall with a power-grabbing principal, the challenge remains great for them. That is, to process those realities, it is likely that the sentiment of Dewey (1964a) resounds at the forefront of their thinking, knowing that a teacher "is not like a private soldier in an army, expected merely to obey, or like a cog in a wheel, expected merely to respond to and transmit external energy" (205). In other words, as Dewey underscores, a teacher is one who intelligently considers his/her action, and has no compunction to criticize or call out "the general principles upon which the whole educational system is formed and administered" (205).

To mitigate the possibilities of that friction, therefore, the school system and, more specifically, the principal, must work toward fostering optimal conditions that cultivate a more meaningful climate of teacher leadership, in which assigning titles is not so much of great concern, but rather an intentional eye on the varied gifts and talents of teachers within the school is the focus. To state differently, the label "teacher" is quite powerful in and of itself, and fundamental to the illumination of their leadership is one in which the teacher routinely exudes competence, credibility, and approachability in their practice (Katzenmeyer and Moller 2009).

The recognition of these three essential elements is clear, present, and experienced by students, their parents/caregivers, colleagues, and the administration. Embedded within the radiation of those elements, it is worthy to emphasize that enthusiasm, persuasiveness, flexibility, confidence, and decisiveness ought to be apparent (Danielson 2007), and that integrity, honesty, and professional ethics ground their thinking, implying that "teacher-leaders are not just good teachers; they are good people" (Merideth 2007, 11).

Thus, in that light, within a setting that values democratic processes, it is these teachers in particular whose voices demand respect in meaningfully participating toward moving a school, and even a school system, forward when it comes to curriculum, policy, and overall direction. As Bowman (2004) puts it, "successful teachers as leaders are adept at influencing constituencies over which they admittedly have no formal authority" (187).

To be sure, what is being suggested here is the notion of shared power or shared governance, one in which school-system administrators do not so much think and act hierarchically, but rather think and act horizontally (or communally) in being more authentically inclusive in placing teachers at the seat of the decision-making table. Creating a community in which democratic spaces are valued clearly demands courage from the principal and teachers to constructively co-exist in the sharing of power, demanding a commitment which involves time, energy, trust, and a collaborative effort (Katzenmeyer and Moller 2009, 2001).

While the model of building a professional community in a school setting where democratic processes are its cornerstone is not a new idea; it is a concept, like teacher leadership, that continues to unfold regarding what it looks like in practice in the context of a hierarchal system. And yet despite our stumbling through that identity process, it is true that teacher leadership, the fostering of collegial collaborative efforts, and the building of professional communities is linked to student achievement and school improvement (Sahlberg 2011; Hargreaves and Shirley 2009; Katzenmeyer and Moller 2009; Danielson 2007; Donaldson Jr. 2007; Lieberman and Friedrich 2007; Merideth 2007; Reeves 2007; Bezzina 2006; Fullan 2006, 2001; Murphy 2005).

AWARENESS AND INVOLVEMENT ARE IMPERATIVE

In the end, teacher leaders naturally emerge in a school setting as evidenced through the distinction they pedagogically demonstrate, the authentic dispositional commitment they exhibit, and the energy they radiate to inspire and challenge others. And to be sure, their leadership extends outside the confines of a school setting, not only by staying aware of the policies and decisions that have an impact on their practice, but also by actively challenging those policies and decisions that may be developmentally inappropriate, unjust, and not mindful of the common good.

Giroux (2011) puts it this way, arguing for an educated hope that "demands that educators become more attentive to the ways in which institutional forces and cultural power are tangled up with everyday experience" (123). In short, teacher leadership requires one to be "socially conscious and politically involved" (Wynne 2001, 3). And that involvement is acutely imperative in an era where powerful forces are at work to dismantle public education, where the importance of teacher preparation is being minimized, and where poverty is an ever-present concern.

TWENTY-SIX

Teacher Leadership and the Greatest Challenge: Poverty

> *Public education is not broken. It is not failing or declining. The diagnosis is wrong, and the solutions of the corporate reformers are wrong. Our urban schools are in trouble because of concentrated poverty and racial segregation.*
>
> (Ravitch 2013, 4)

In the United States, eclipsing that of many industrialized nations, 14.8 percent (46.7 million) of Americans live in poverty, and nearly twenty-one million live in extreme poverty, meaning living on an income that is below half of the poverty line (approximately twelve thousand dollars per year for a family of four). Moreover, particularly for the African American and Latino population, the poverty rate significantly exceeds the national average. Finally, since 2007, the poverty rate for children has gone from 18 percent to 21.1 percent (15.5 million) (U.S. Census Bureau 2014). Without question, the likely negative impact for children who live in poverty is great in comparison to those who do not.

Among other negative consequences, children who live in poverty are more likely to experience (Moore et al. 2009):

- Low birth weight, food insecurity (i.e. not having enough to eat, poor diet, parents' inability to consistently purchase adequate, nutritious food);
- Chronic health ailments such as asthma and anemia;
- Living in substandard housing, being raised by parents/caregivers with minimal years of formal education;
- Living in households with little cognitive stimulation, negatively impacting cognitive and academic success;
- A greater risk of manifesting inappropriate behavior, disobedience, impulsiveness, emotional issues, and poor peer interaction;

- Exposure to parental substance abuse, violent crime, environmental toxins, and minimal-quality child care services;
- Living in substandard, unsafe neighborhoods;
- Subjection to frequent moves, family structure changes; and
- Poverty as an adult.[1]

To that end, poverty is not only about economic state, but about other factors listed above, it also severely handcuffs one from fully participating in the community. In other words, as Nouwen (1983) insightfully states, "poverty is so much more than lack of money, lack of food, or lack of decent living quarters. Poverty creates marginal people, people who are separated from that whole network of ideas, services, facilities and opportunities" (118).

MARKETIZATION OF EDUCATION WORKS TO ALIENATE

Addressing the critical concern of poverty and arriving at some resolution is multifaceted and complex, to be sure. Economic injustice, a system of capitalism that inherently exploits, and an education system that creates "winners" and "losers" are all part of the discourse.[2] With respect to the latter, what is profoundly needed is an education system that is just, equitable, developmentally appropriate, culturally relevant, and engaging for all students, but particularly for those who have been for too long on the outside looking in.

The problem, however, is that the current U.S. education system, as was earlier discussed in this text, with its market model approach to schooling, its link to standardized testing, and its attack on public-school teachers, is by and large further alienating the very "at-risk" population it purports to help. In fact, responding to the easy target of many who declare that what ails public education is incompetent teachers, Ravitch (2010) rejects that claim—although those who fall into that category should be appropriately handled—and asserts that the problem and the challenge is poverty.

One thing is clear with respect to education: a more holistic, visionary solution than that espoused by corporate so-called reformers is clearly needed. Indeed, the marketization of education has reduced teachers into mechanical functionaries, seriously handcuffing them from fostering critical thought, innovation, and the cultivation to inculcate the love of learning. This translates into a learning environment that heavily relies on what Freire (1990) calls a banking approach, propagating a silver-bullet, one-size-fits-all prescription of what "successful" teaching and learning is, while at the same time trivializing the complex psychological, physical, cognitive, cultural, emotional, and economic impact of poverty.

School-aged young people in poverty do not need to be "saved" from their "condition" with a prescription that simply has domestication as its aim. Rather, school-aged youngsters from poverty—like all youngsters—need to be understood; need to explore; need to be listened to; need to discuss the very conditions that create poverty; need to engage in critical dialogue; need exposure to diversity of thought, knowledge, and disciplines; need the arts; need to be encouraged, loved, and challenged; need a structured and unstructured environment; need to be evaluated and assessed through multiple media; need competent, engaging, creative, well-prepared teachers; and especially need what Freire (1990) calls a problem-posing approach to teaching and learning.[3]

Reflecting on the social, economic, and educational landscape in the United States, Jonathan Kozol (1995) states, "things that are wrong, are wrong in such obvious ways. We lack the moral and theological will to act on what we already know" (4C). And though Kozol's words were stated over twenty years ago, they are perhaps more urgent now than when he first uttered them.

Indeed, educational reform is *not* what is needed in order to respond to Kozol's rhetorical question as to whether or not we have the moral and theological will to act on what we know about the things that are obviously wrong. That is, the word "reform" only implies change or modification, yet maintains the fundamental infrastructure of the system.

Thus, it is worth repeating: education reform is *not* what is needed; rather, what *is* needed is revolutionary, transformative change of the infrastructure of the system itself. A critical step in advancing that end is for teacher leaders to courageously rise up and to be transformative agents toward leading that change.

ENTER IN CRITICAL PEDAGOGY

Accordingly, teacher leaders are those who are critical pedagogues, and critical pedagogues are those who have a fundamental grasp of critical pedagogy. While there are multiple descriptions as to what critical pedagogy is, there are, however, central characteristics that are woven throughout all explanations of critical pedagogy.

That is, critical pedagogy is theoretically grounded; realizes that there is no such thing as a neutral education; is aware of the political nature of education; does not look at education and life itself from a reductionistic or a deterministic point of view; seeks to comprehend the link between knowledge and power; is contextually attentive; promotes human rights, justice, and democracy; is a process of transformation; is a way of thinking; pays attention to gender, class, race, and ethnicity issues and its relationship to oppression/liberation; moves both teacher and student in a horizontal relationship as subjects; challenges the status quo; and is continuously evolving (Kirylo 2011).

In short, the thinking of critical pedagogy provides perceptive insight to not only understand disparities and injustices in education, but also offers an incisive language to explain marginalization, alienation, and oppression, ultimately guiding the opening of the proverbial door to transformative solutions in fostering an authentic education that is democratic, just, and inclusive. In short, the notion of critical pedagogy offers a path to walk in hope and provides a frame through which educators can move toward that attentive activism in fostering a more humanizing world, one that works to make a preferential option for the poor.

The notion of preferential option for the poor is a central theme that drives what is known as liberation theology, which is a spiritual way of viewing reality from the perspective of the poor and marginalized. As Jezreel (1997) contends, "a preferential option for the poor simply reminds us who we are: a people who, when we are honest and awake, would do anything to end one another's suffering" (35).

Utilizing theology and the social sciences, liberation theology calls for faith and action to foster the progress of the oppressed, the poor, the infirmed, and the marginalized (Boff and Boff 1984). Moreover, liberation theology reminds us that if we are to have an emancipatory system of schooling whereby the poor and marginalized are to become a meaningful part of the official story, then we must consider the notion of making a preferential option for those who have historically found themselves on the outside looking in (Kincheloe 1992).

In the end, over the last several decades, civic and religious leaders have continuously asserted that a fundamental moral test of a just society is how its most vulnerable members are faring, and that "option for the poor" is fundamental to a life-giving, productive society (National Conference of Catholic Bishops 1995, 1994, 1986).[4]

IMMERSED IN THE COMMUNITY

In that traditional space called a classroom, critical educators have a unique responsibility to be mindful of the notion that pedagogy is perpetually joined at the hip with forces related to the economic, social, and political sphere (Giroux 2011, 2007). And where economic injustice is evident, where violations of human rights are occurring, where equal access and opportunity have been subverted, and where freedoms have been violated, teacher leaders should not only examine the impact this has on students and society as a whole, but they should also act with an honorable anger and with what Darder (2002) characterizes as a "pedagogy of love" (30).

In the final analysis, teacher leaders are not only those who demonstrate profound competence within their classroom, but are also those who remain immersed in their communities; and where inequality is perpetrated, they resist, take courage, and act, encouraging the entire village to be involved.

NOTES

1. There is no doubt regarding the monumental effect of poverty on young people, with implications that are varied, multifaceted, and complex. This is not to say, however, that despite the impact of poverty, many young people heroically and resiliently rise above their circumstances through the combinational efforts of wide-ranging support systems such as good parenting and encouraging family structures; through the support of the faith community; through the support of mentors; through the support of governmental intervention; through the support of good schools; through the support of quality after-school programs; and a host of other entities. Indeed, it takes a family to raise a child, but as will be discussed in the final chapter, it also takes a village to pave the road in order to enable a child's growth.

2. As Freire (1998b) notes, capitalism is a system founded on "its intrinsic perversity, its antisolidarity nature . . . It has produced scarcity within abundance and need within plenty" (88).

3. As opposed to a banking approach to education which is driven by the assumptions that people are manageable and adaptable, reality is compartmentalized, static, and predictable, and students essentially learn through memorization, a problem-posing approach is one that assumes people are conscious beings who are unfinished but in the process of becoming and that learning occurs through in a dialogical environment (Freire 1990).

4. For a succinct explanation of liberation theology and preferential option for the poor, among other sources, see Kirylo (2006, 2001) and Jezreel (1997).

TWENTY-SEVEN

It Takes a Village

> *What the best and wisest parent wants for his own child, that must the community want for all of its children. Any other ideal for our schools is narrow and unlovely; acted upon, it destroys our democracy.*
>
> (Dewey 1943, 6–7)

While genetics play a part in the shaping of personality traits, temperament, and development, and while children are born into a cross-section of income brackets, races, ethnicities, and family structures, all children are born on a playing field where "there is no achievement gap at birth" (Delpit 2012, 3). And that, of course, is the point.

A newborn has no choice in what station s/he is born; society, however, has a choice as to what kind of community that infant will greet. As has been established in section II of this book, the human family fundamentally strives and prospers in relationships. In fact, "our greatest gift is to connect, and we function better in connection as individuals and as a society" (A. Banks 2010).

Particularly at a school setting where there is a genuine focus on realizing the power of cultivating harmonious relationships among educators, students, and parents, the research is overwhelming regarding the positive impact these relationships have on fostering professional growth, effective teaching and meaningful learning, student voice, student engagement, student well-being, enjoyment of school, achievement, improvement, success, and the overall transformation of schools (Quinn and Owen 2014; Jacobs 2012; Spilt, Koomen, and Thijs 2011; Kersey and Masterson 2009; Lewis 2008; Witmer 2005; Klem and Connell 2004; Mitra 2003; Bryk and Schneider 2003; Hoffman and Levak 2003).

The challenge, however—in a culture where we place a high premium on "the rugged individual" at the expense of downplaying the significance of connecting with one another (A. Banks 2010)—is qualitatively and genuinely realizing the critical importance of relationships. In fact, particularly in an era of rigid standardization and a warped sense of what is meant by accountability where schools, administrators, and teachers are more and more intensely judged based on whether students pass tests or not, the importance of relationships has become increasingly minimized, resulting in a cold corporatized climate that predominately concentrates on product, outcome, and competition.

This coldness has dictated political platforms whereby politicians manipulatively, callously, and even ignorantly use certain school statistics in whatever ways that suit their platforms; it has placed parents/caregivers in a place of fear, unduly placing pressure on their children to "perform"; it has led students to drop out, check out, to be disillusioned and disengaged with school, and has caused educators to become peculiarly prescriptive in their approach.[1] Finally, much of this bureaucratic coldness of what schooling is about is being conveyed by the media, perversely shaping public opinion about what is important in education (Kirylo and Nauman 2006).

On that latter score, Lakoff (2004) argues that to reframe, and ultimately change the discourse surrounding any complex and contested terrain (such as school happenings) requires a changing of the language used to describe and talk about that terrain, underscoring that a big part of that reframing effort falls in the hands of the media. In other words, "reframing is not just about words and language. Reframing is about ideas. The ideas have to be in place in people's brains before the sound bite can make any sense" (Lakoff 2004, 105).

Hancock (2005) echoes Lakoff, arguing that the newspaper media, particularly those who conduct school reporting, should become more intimately informed regarding the complexities of schooling and the limitations of standardization, and to probe deeper, and to report more carefully regarding the happenings in school systems and in schools. However, it is obviously not only the media, but the entire community (i.e., civic, religious, and cultural leaders, etc.) that has a civic responsibility to probe deeper and to be more informed regarding the happenings in education.

And within that probing, one may realize the opportunity given to the community that indeed "there is no achievement gap at birth." And particularly relevant for those who have been historically disenfranchised, have lacked opportunity, have been viewed with low expectations, and have had to confront bigotry, prejudice, racism, and all other forms of discrimination and inequality, the entire community, the village, must come together in a collective voice in realizing the power and importance of connection, relationships, and the movement toward change.

CONCLUSION

When Hillary Rodham Clinton (1996) rightly claims that "children are not rugged individuals" (7), she is not only implying that they depend on their parents, who are foremost responsible in caring and raising that child; she is also implying that the community in which that child is born bears responsibility as well, simply because the adults in the community are the ones who are daily making civic decisions related to education, health care, social services, and so on, all of which has an impact on the children in the community. As Clinton argues, "the true test of the consensus we build is how well we care for our children. For a child, the village must remain personal . . . How well we care for our own and other people's children isn't only a question of morality; our self-interest is at stake too" (15).

Achievement gaps are a socially constructed phenomena; and so, while there are a host of interrelated reasons, these gaps are chiefly a result of a lack of opportunity, resources, authentic commitment, and misguided community decisions. And when Comer (2004) reminds us that education is about relationships, relationships, relationships, he is simultaneously saying that the current way of doing things is off kilter, and is in fact contributing to the gaps in achievement. Comer (2004) proclaims it this way: "The inappropriate models and emphases now used to shape education practice, evaluation and policies, and the mentalities and behaviors they generate are themselves a big part of education crises" (7).

So, there we have it. The question then becomes: What is the village going to do about it? Do we have the courage to collectively rise above our petty politics and to rest our egos that are in overdrive and come together as a community to recognize the ultimate importance of connection, particularly for our young people? Do we have the will to create schooling environments in which opportunity abounds for *all*, developmentally appropriate practices are common place for *all*, and where *all* naturally curious youngsters are recognized for their individual beauties, gifts, and talents? And while we see pockets of substantive direction in which our young people are immersed in rich schooling environments, those and other questions continue to loom large.

To that end—when it comes to the institutional infrastructure of education—in our continuing efforts toward maximizing opportunity, toward fostering developmentally appropriate practices, toward tapping into the natural curiosities of our school-aged youth, and toward making meaningful human connections, an excellent cornerstone for the village to rest its foundation is looking toward the educator who teaches with purpose. For teachers who authentically understand the who and why they teach; who are contextually aware; who are clear about the critical aspects of teaching, and think globally, but act locally, the entire community will radiate toward the direction of purposeful educational transformation.

NOTE

1. Foster (2008) would characterize these educators as "helicopter teachers," implying they are suffocating students in the strict manner in which they themselves are following the exact prescribed curriculum, leaving no room for creativity, risk-taking, or creative exploration. The idea of "helicopter teachers" is played off from the idea of "helicopter parents," who are parents who are generally characterized as overprotective, regularly "hovering" around teachers, and somewhat detrimental in allowing a child to grow in independence in a school setting.

Appendix A

DERIVATIVE AND HISTORICAL UNFOLDING OF INSPIRATION

The word "inspiration" is a derivative of the Latin *inspirare*, meaning to inflame or breathe into, even suggesting "God-breathed," or breathed into by the divine. More formally, Merriam-Webster (2012) includes the following in its definition of inspiration:

(1) a: divine influence or action on a person believed to qualify him or her to receive and communicate sacred revelation; b: the action or power of moving the intellect or emotions; c: the act of influencing or suggesting opinions; (2) the act of drawing in; *specif*: the drawing of air into the lungs; (3) a: the quality or state of being inspired; b: something that is inspired (a scheme that was pure inspiration); (4) an inspiring agent or influence.

In sum, Merriam-Webster's formal articulation combined with the variety of other definitions that exist demonstrate that inspiration is a phenomenon that naturally intersects with the spiritual, emotional, psychological, physical, and the cognitive, and that provokingly is associated with such sensations as to affect, to arouse, to induce, to enliven, to stimulate, to guide, to imbue, to influence, and to touch.

If we take a bird's-eye view back in examining the historical unfolding of inspiration as a recognized happening, we learn that one of the initial manifestations of it was experienced by the poet-seers of the *Rigveda*, which is a sacred Hindu text comprised of hymns, praises, and prayers that dates back approximately to 1100 B.C. Known as the *rishis*, these poet-seers would implore the gods for inspiration for the composition of their text (Carpenter 1987).

During the Gupta Period (320–550 CE) or what is also known as the classical age in India, the Sanskrit poeticians were thought to be imbued with what is known as *pratibhā* or inspiration, which sparked their poetic imagination (Shulman 2008), and in ancient Greece poets drew creative inspiration from the Muses (nine goddesses or daughters of Zeus) where Plato describes the inspirational process as a type of mania that propelled their (poets') utterances (Hart 1998; Carpenter 1987).

Disciples in early Mahāyāna Buddhism were thought to be inspired in spontaneous praise of Buddha, and in Hinduism, a practice or movement called *bhakti* (devotion, to share, to love) emerged in the seventh century where followers are said to be inspired in their poetry and hymns to the gods Visnu and Śiva. In the Jewish and Christian tradition, there has been a natural traditional role of inspiration. For the former, the rabbinical idea of *ruach hakodesh* (denoting the Spirit of Yahweh) was appropriated to elucidate the notion of divine prophetic inspiration, and for the latter, the nurturing of inspiration is a result of the outpouring of the Holy Spirit on believers. Muhammad, a critical prophet in the Islamic tradition—profoundly shaping political, social, and religious belief worldwide—is recognized as an inspired prophet of God or the last of the prophets of God (Carpenter 1987).

LINKED TO ENTHUSIASM, CREATIVITY, AND MOTIVATION

The notion of inspiration, as described above, is associated with supernatural happenings of some sort; moreover, it implicitly possesses an intimate link with the human sense or sensation of enthusiasm. That is, enthusiasm comes from the Latin *enthūsiasmus*, which comes from the Greek *enthousiasmos*, inferring possession by a god who inspires creation, imagination, and utterings (Hart 1998).

While the concept of inspiration assumes a natural historical tie to the world of religion, faith, and spirituality, this is not to suggest, however, that the explanation (or even the experience) of it is limited to the language of that realm, or is not relevant to the "secular," or is only reserved for a select few (Hart 2000).

Particularly emerging during the latter stages of the nineteenth century, the discipline of psychology examined inspiration through an intrapsychic (within the mind) lens, viewing it deterministically as opposed to supernaturally, focusing on the creative instead of the religious, and emphasizing illumination that arises from the psyche instead of divine revelation (Thrash and Elliot 2003). Erupting from within, inspiration can provoke a reaction in an individual that can be marked in its suddenness and impersonality. For the former, Ribot (1973) puts it this way:

> It [inspiration] makes a sudden eruption into consciousness, but one presupposing a latent, frequently long, labor. It has its analogous among other well-known psychic states; for example, a passion that is forgotten, which, after a long period of incubation, reveals itself through an act; or, better, a sudden resolve after endless deliberation which did not seem able to come to a head . . . Sometimes, indeed, inspiration bursts forth in deep sleep and awakens the sleeper, and lest we may suppose this suddenness to be especially characteristic of artists we see it in all forms of invention. (52)

For the latter, the concept of the impersonal nature of inspiration is driven by the idea that an unknown power source greater than the conscious individual moves through one to act (e.g., invent, create, compose).

While those with a spiritual bent to their thinking would perhaps characterize that power source as that related to the otherworldly, others not of that persuasion may see that inspired action as one "derived from the unconscious activity of the mind" (Ribot 1973, 53). Building on the thinking of Freud, it is also theorized that inspiration emerges from the preconscious, which is that unique place that provides the stream that bridges the gulf between the subconscious and conscious. Inspiration that is moved either by the unconscious or conscious can certainly be prompted by some outside environmental factors such as nature, poetry, art, mentors, role models, and a number of other externals (Thrash and Elliot 2003).

According to Hart (2000), inspiration—from across all cultures and throughout time and whether its source is perceived to be spiritual in nature or from some kind of heightened brain activity—is a distinct, epistemologically nonrational happening that occurs often unexpectedly and quite markedly dissimilar from ordinary waking consciousness, fostering acute illumination, awareness, knowing, and understanding. As Hart (2000) asserts:

> Inspiration is the poet in the process of learning, the prophet beholding the voice of God, the artist hearing the Muse, and the "ordinary" person becoming, if only for a moment, extraordinary . . . Inspiration emerged as a birdsong for Milton, like a dream for van Gogh, a song for Goethe, a flash of light for Tchaikovsky, a beneficent power for Dickens, as a golden chain linking earth and heaven for Homer, and as love for Dante. (33)

It is true that the literature is scant that examines inspiration and its relationship to psychology, but the likely reason for this is because inspiration has more often been linked with the phenomenon of creativity and motivation (Degaard 2005; Thrash and Elliot 2004; Hart 2000).

Not unlike our conceptual understanding of inspiration, creativity is a cognitive process that somewhat possesses an enigmatic flavor, yet we know it is significantly linked to such concepts as illumination, inspiration, imagination, ingenuity, insight, intuition, originality, and innovation (Henry 1991).

In fact, Csikszentmihalyi (1996) compellingly argues that the fostering of creativity is central in making sense of our lives because "most of the things that are interesting, important, and *human* are the results of creativity" (1). Csikszentmihalyi goes on to underscore that a natural outcome of our engagement in creative endeavors suggests living more meaningful lives. May (1975) further suggests that one fulfills one's being in the world through the manifestations of one's creativity.

While the concept of motivation is further touched on in chapter 17, it is clear that it is associated with creativity and our understanding of inspiration (Csikszentmihalyi 1996; Henry 1991; McAleer 1991). Moreover, where inspiration can be viewed as the illumination, "aha" moment, energy surge, spark, or catalyst for a thought or project, motivation acts as the operational unfolding intent or pragmatic plan in sustaining a focus to realizing our goals (Hart 2000). To succinctly make the point regarding a venture that is inspirationally sparked, Henry (1991) notes, "As the saying goes, it's 98% perspiration and 2% inspiration" (10), or as Ward (1970) puts it, "Inspiration is often the brain child of perspiration and concentration" (55).

Appendix B

A RESPONSE TO THE TYLERIAN RATIONALE

While Tyler's influence on curriculum development cannot be ignored, the postmodern curriculum development paradigm, which hones in on the autobiographical narrative, challenges the traditional Tylerian model (Slattery 1995). Beginning in the 1970s, a powerful movement to reconceptualize the meaning and action of curriculum flowered as a result of, among the scholarship of others, William Pinar's etymological examination of *currere*, the Latin infinitive verb of the word "curriculum" (Pinar et al. 1995; Pinar and Grumet 1976).

Pinar compellingly questions the traditional way in which curriculum is viewed, arguing that the term has been misunderstood (Slattery 1995), and as pointed out in chapter 13 of this text, *currere* implies to run the racecourse, meaning that curriculum is not seen as something tangible, as in the case of the articulation of goals and objectives. Rather, curriculum is an activity, an inward autobiographical journey, impacting direction of the schooling experience. In other words, curriculum work must be historically contextualized, explored, and negotiated, all of which must be linked to conceptions of emancipation (Giroux 1988).

In the end, curriculum is more than the disciplines, the setting of goals and objectives, or the number of prescribed minutes per study of subject matter. Rather, the reconceptualization of curriculum includes concepts related to the dialectical nature of becoming, concepts related to power, and the favoring or nonfavoring of respective forms of knowledge, ultimately linked to critical pedagogy, which finds its theoretical understandings in critical theory.

Appendix C

A SAMPLING OF PARENTAL VOICE AND TESTING

While numerous illustrations can be given from all over the country regarding the stress and anxiety standardized testing has created, the following is but a few testimonies.

Regarding his two sons, a Denver, Colorado parent shares his story on standardized tests, explaining the following:

> Each year, around testing time, he noticed a change in his kids. They came home demoralized, with shoulders slumped and heads down. "No joy in what they're doing, no joy in education," said Prather. And after the tests were over, it seemed that instruction mostly ceased for the remainder of the year . . .
>
> Top administrators in Dougco, the state's third-largest district, recently called the amount of testing "madness" and said students, at some level, are taking mandated tests almost every day of the year. Superintendent Liz Fagen skewered the overuse of standardized tests on the district's website earlier this fall, saying they measure low-level skills and create a "focus on mediocrity." In Denver, outgoing school board member Andrea Merida attributed her decision not to run for reelection in part to her belief that "high-stakes standardized testing is destroying public education today."[1]

From a report in Cleveland, Ohio, a parent, Mandy Jablonski, shared the following, saying:

> Her fifth-grade son won't be taking any state tests this year. Jablonski said her son was so sick with nausea and dizziness last spring that she took him to several doctors for blood and vision tests, even an MRI. Doctors couldn't figure it out. He felt better, Jablonski said, when his school in Elyria finished taking state tests. That experience convinced her that he would not take tests any more.
>
> Brusky told an Ohio House hearing on Common Core that the response from the Amherst school district when she decided to pull her son out of tests showed just how much of a premium schools put on testing. First, school officials suggested that she have her son take some medication on test days for his anxiety. "The principal told me that I would hurt the school, hurt the district and he pointed to the teachers and said, 'Do you know how bad you will hurt the teachers if your son doesn't take the test?'"[2]

In a story from New York:

> Some parents have just said no to standardized tests . . . Parents from several schools rallied in Harlem to announce they were opting out of Common Core tests for their children. They held signs reading, "more teaching, more art, more gym, and less testing." "We need to stand up and we need to let the New York State Education Department know that that is enough," said Jasmine Batista, a parent of a third and fifth grader. Parents claim too much time is spent on test prep at the expense of learning. Donnie Rotkin, who has been teaching for thirty years and is now an instructional coach, said schools have become so test-centric they have distorted learning.[3]

Finally from a story in Royal Palm Beach, Florida:

> One parent reported that her third-grade son comes home from school every day thinking he is stupid because he can't pass his tests. "Mommy, please home-school me," he begged.[4]

NOTES

1. co.chalkbeat.org/2013/11/19/amid-angst-over-standardized-tests-some-parents-say-no-thanks/#.VE53VpB0waI.

2. www.cleveland.com/metro/index.ssf/2014/10/test_mania_parents_opt_out_of.html.

3. newyork.cbslocal.com/2014/03/27/some-nyc-parents-say-their-kids-are-opting-out-of-common-core-tests/.

4. reason.com/blog/2014/10/20/kids-react-to-common-core-mommy-please-h.

References

Aldridge, J., and Goldman, R. (2002). *Current issues and trends in education.* Boston: Allyn and Bacon.

Ayers, W. (2005). "Education for a changing world." In D. A. Breault and R. Breault, eds. *Experiencing Dewey: Insights for today's classroom* (second edition). Indianapolis, IN: Kappa Delta Pi International Honor Society in Education.

Ayers, W. (1993). *To teach: The journey of a teacher.* New York: Teachers College Press.

Ball, D. L., and McDiarmid, G. W. (1990). "The subject-matter preparation of teachers." In W. R. Houston, M. Haberman, and J. Sikula, eds., *Handbook of research on teacher education: A project of the Association of Teacher Educators.* New York: Macmillan Publishing Company, 437–49.

Bandura, A. (1986). *Social foundations of thought and action: A social-cognitive theory.* Englewood Cliffs, NJ: Prentice-Hall.

Banks, A. (2010). "Humans are hardwired for connection? Neurobiology 101 for parents, educators, and the general public." *Jean Baker Miller Training Institute at Wellesley Centers for Women.* Retrieved from http://www.jbmti.org/Media-Coverage/humans-are-hardwired-for-connection-neurobiology-101-for-parents-educators-a-the-general-public.

Banks, J. A. (2014). "Series foreword". In C. A. Torres, *First Freire: Early writings in social justice education.* New York: Teachers College Press.

Banks, J. A. (2010). "Series foreword". In J. W. Loewen, *Teaching what really happened: How to avoid the tyranny of textbooks and get students excited about doing history.* New York: Teachers College Press, ix–xiii.

Banks, J. A. (2006). *Cultural diversity and education: Foundations, curriculum, and teaching* (fifth edition). Boston: Pearson Education.

Banner, J., and Cannon, H. (1997). *The elements of teaching.* New Haven, CT: Yale University Press.

Barone, T. (1983). "Education as aesthetic experience: 'Art in gem.'" *Educational Leadership,* 40(4), 21–26. Retrieved from http://www.ascd.org/publications/educational-leadership/jan83/vol40/num04/toc.aspx.

Barth, R. S. (2006). "Improving relationships within the schoolhouse." *Educational Leadership,* 63(6), 9–13.

Bennett, C. I. (2007). *Comprehensive multicultural education: Theory and practice* (sixth edition). Boston: Pearson Education.

Berliner, D. C., and Biddle, B. J. (1995). *The manufactured crisis: Myths, fraud, and the attack on America's public schools.* New York: Perseus Books.

Bertrand, A., and Cebula, J. P. (1980). *Tests, measurement, and evaluation: A developmental approach.* Reading, MA: Addison-Wesley Publishing Company.

Bezzina, C. (2006). "'The road less traveled': Professional communities in secondary schools." *Theory into Practice* 45(2), 159–67.

Black, P. J. (1998). *Testing: Friend or foe?* London: The Falmer Press.

Blight, D. W. (2010). "Afterword". In D. Eltis and D. Richardson, *Atlas of the Transatlantic Slave Trade.* New Haven, CT: Yale University Press, 291–97.

Boff, C., and Boff, L. (1984). *Salvation and liberation: In search of a balance between faith and politics* R. R. Barr, trans. Maryknoll, NY: Orbis Books.

Bowman, R. F. (2004). "Teachers as leaders". *The Clearing House* 77(5), 187–89.

Bowman, Jr., R. F. (2007) "How can students be motivated: A misplaced question?" In *The Clearing House: A Journal of Educational Strategies, Issues and Ideas* 81(2), 81–86.

Bowman, S. (2014). *Number of standardized tests public-school students take exploded in past decade*. Retrieved from http://www.islandpacket.com/2014/03/30/3026373/education-testing-day-2.html?sp=/99/100/andihp=1.
Bryk, A. S. and Schneider, B. (2003). "Trust in schools: A core resource for school reform." *Educational Leadership* 60(6), 40–45.
Buber, M. (1958). *I and thou* (second edition). New York: Scribner.
Burkett, J. A. (2013). *Teacher perception on differentiated instruction and its influence on instructional practice* (doctoral dissertation). Retrieved from ProQuest Dissertations and Theses. (1427918798).
Cahn, S. M. (1970). *The philosophical foundations of education*. New York: Harper and Row.
Cameron, W. B. (1963). *Informal sociology: A casual introduction to sociological thinking*. New York: Random House.
Campbell, E. (2003). *The ethical teacher*. Maidenhead, UK: Open University Press.
Carpenter, D. (1987). "Inspiration". In M. Eliade, ed., *The encyclopedia of religion*. New York: Macmillan, 256–59.
Carroll, D. (2007). "Developing dispositions for ambitious teaching." *Journal of Educational Controversy*, 2(2). Retrieved from http://www.wce.wwu.edu/Resources/CEP/eJournal/v002n002/.
Casbergue, R. M. (2013). "Lev Semenovich Vygotsky: The Mozart of psychology." In J. D. Kirylo, ed. *A critical pedagogy of resistance: 34 pedagogues we need to know*. Rotterdam, The Netherlands: Sense Publications, 125–28.
Charles, C. M. (2008). *Building classroom discipline* (ninth edition). White Plains, NY: Allyn and Bacon.
Chomsky, N. (2015). *Noam Chomsky on the dangers of standardized testing*. Retrieved from creativesystemsthinking.wordpress.com/2015/02/21/noam-chomsky-on-the-dangers-of-standardized-testing/.
Cizek, G. J., and Burg, S. S. (2006). *Addressing test anxiety in a high-stakes environment: Strategies for classrooms and schools*. Thousand Oaks, CA: Corwin Press.
Clinton, H. R. (1996). *It takes a village: And other lessons children teach us*. New York: Simon and Schuster.
Collett, J. L., Kelly, S., and Sobolewski, C. (2010). "Using remember the titans to teach theories of conflict reduction." *Teaching Sociology* 38(3), 258–66.
Collins, D. E. (1977). *Paulo Freire: His life, works and thought*. New York: Paulist Press.
Comer, J. (2004). *Leave no child behind: Preparing today's youth for tomorrow's world*. New Haven, CT: Yale University Press.
Cooperstein, S., and Kocevar-Weidinger, E. (2004). "Beyond active learning: A constructivist approach to learning." *Reference Services Review* 32(2), 141–48.
Costa, A. L., and Kallick, B. (2000). "Preface to the series". In A. L. Costa and B. Kallick, eds. *Discovering and exploring habits of mind*. Alexandria, VA: Association for Supervision and Curriculum Development, xii–xvi.
Cozolino, L. (2013). *The social neuroscience of education: Optimizing attachment and learning in the classroom*. New York: W. W. Norton and Company.
Crain, W. (2000). *Theories of development: Concepts and applications* (fourth edition). Upper Saddle River, NJ: Prentice Hall.
Csikszentmihalyi, M. (1996). *Creativity: Flow and the psychology of discovery and invention*. New York: HarperCollins.
Cummins, J. (2008). "Foreword". In S. Nieto and P. Bode, *Affirming Diversity: The sociopolitical context of multicultural education* (fifth edition). Boston: Pearson Education, xiv–xvii.
Cushner, K., McClelland, A., and Safford, P. (2012). *Human diversity in education: An intercultural approach* (seventh edition). New York: McGraw-Hill.
Danforth, S., and Boyle, J. (2007). *Cases in behavior management* (second edition). Columbus, OH: Allyn and Bacon/Merrill.
Danielson, C. (2007). "The many faces of leadership". *Educational Leadership* 65(1), 14–19.

Danielson, C., and Abrutyn, L. (1997). *An introduction to using portfolios in the classroom.* Alexandria, VA: Association for Supervision and Curriculum Development.

Darder, A. (2002). *Reinventing Paulo Freire: A pedagogy of love.* Boulder, CO: Westview Press.

Darling-Hammond, L. (2006a). "Constructing 21st-century teacher education". *Journal of Teacher Education* 57(3), 300–14.

Darling-Hammond, L. (2006b). *Powerful teacher education: Lessons from exemplary programs.* San Francisco, CA: Jossey-Bass.

Darling-Hammond, L. (2004). "From 'separate but equal' to 'no child left behind': The collision of new standards and old inequalities." In D. Meier and G. Wood, eds. *Many children left behind: How the No Child Left Behind Act is damaging our children and our schools.* Boston: Beacon Press, 3–32.

Darling-Hammond, L. (1997). *The right to learn: A blueprint for creating schools that work.* San Francisco, CA: Jossey-Bass.

Davis, D. B. (2010). "Foreword". In D. Eltis and D. Richardson, *Atlas of the Transatlantic Slave Trade.* New Haven, CT: Yale University Press, xvii–xxii.

Degaard, F. M. (2005). *The inspiration process: Its source and its role* (unpublished doctoral dissertation). Garden City, NY: Adelphi University.

Deiro, J. (1997). "Teacher strategies for nurturing healthy connections with students". *Journal for a Just and Caring Education,* 3(2), 192–202.

Delpit, L. (2012). *"Multiplication is for white people": Raising expectations for other people's children.* New York: The New Press.

Dewey, J. (1983). *The middle works of John Dewey, 1899–1924,* Vol. 14. J. A. Boydston, ed. Carbondale and Edwardsville: Southern Illinois University Press.

Dewey, J. (1964a). "What psychology can do for the teacher". In R. D. Archambault, ed. *John Dewey on education: Selected writings.* New York, The Modern Library, 195–211.

Dewey, J. (1964b). "My pedagogic creed." In R. D. Archambault, ed. *John Dewey on education: Selected writings.* New York: The Modern Library, 427–39¬.

Dewey, J. (1943). *The school and society* (revised edition). Chicago, IL: The University of Chicago Press.

Dewey, J. (1933). *How we think: A restatement of the relation of reflective thinking to the educative process.* Boston: D. C. Heath and Company.

Dewey, J. (1916). *Democracy and education.* New York: Macmillan.

Dewey, J. (1909). *Moral principles in education.* Boston: Houghton Mifflin Company.

Donaldson Jr., G. A. (2007). "What do teachers bring to leadership?" *Educational Leadership* 65(1), 26–29.

Durnford, V. L. (2010). *An examination of teacher-student trust in middle school classrooms* (unpublished doctoral dissertation). Amherst, MA: University of Massachusetts Amherst.

Eggen, P., and Kauchak, D. (2004). *Educational psychology: Windows on classrooms* (sixth edition). Upper Saddle River, NJ: Pearson Merrill Prentice Hall.

Eginli, I. (2007). *Principal leadership and teacher commitment to the profession: The mediating role of collective efficacy and teacher efficacy* (unpublished doctoral dissertation). Fairfax, VA: George Mason University.

Eisner, E. (2006). "The satisfaction of teaching". *Educational Leadership,* 63(6), 44–45.

Eisner, E. (2002). *The educational imagination: On the design and evaluation of school programs* (third edition). Upper Saddle River, NJ: Merrill Prentice Hall.

Eisner, E. (1991). *The enlightened eye: Qualitative inquiry and the enhancement of educational practice.* New York: Macmillan.

Eisner, E. (n.d.) *The roots of connoisseurship and criticism: A personal journey.* Retrieved from www.sagepub.com/upm-data/47742_alkin2e_ch31and32.pdf.

Eldred, S. (1997). "A touching friendship: Helen Keller and Anne Sullivan". *New Moon* 5(38). Retrieved from http://ezproxy.selu.edu/login?url=http://search.proquest.com/docview/194788345?accountid=13772.

Elkind, D. (2000). "Developmentally appropriate practice: Philosophical and practical implications". In F. W. Parkay and G. Hass, *Curriculum planning: A contemporary approach* (seventh edition). Boston: Allyn and Bacon, 107–14.

Eltis, D., and Richardson, D. (2010). *Atlas of the transatlantic slave trade*. New Haven, CT: Yale University Press.

Fecho, B. (2011). *Teaching for the students: Habits of heart, mind, and practice in the engaged classroom*. New York: Teachers College Press.

Flinders, D. J. (1989). "Does the "art of teaching" have a future?" *Educational Leadership* 46(8), 16–20.

Foster, C. (2008). "Beware the rise of helicopter teachers". *The Times Educational Supplement* (4771), 28. Retrieved from http://ezproxy.selu.edu/login?url=http://search.proquest.com/docview/763621598?accountid=13772.

Fraser, R. J. (2008). *Demystifying teacher leadership in comprehensive high schools* (unpublished doctoral dissertation). Philadelphia: University of Pennsylvania Press.

Freedom Writers, and Gruwell, E. (1999). *The freedom writers diary: How a teacher and 150 teens used writing to change themselves and the world around them*. New York: Broadway Books.

Freire, A., and Vittoria, P. (2007). "Dialogue on Paulo Freire". *Interamerican Journal of Education for Democracy* 1(1), 97–117. Retrieved from www.ried–ijed.org.

Freire, P. (2007). *Daring to dream: Toward a pedagogy of the unfinished* (organized and presented by Ana Maria Araújo Freire). A. K. Oliveira, trans. Boulder, CO: Paradigm Publishers.

Freire, P. (2005). *Teachers as cultural workers: Letters to those who dare teach* (expanded edition). Boulder, CO: Westview Press.

Freire, P. (1998a). *Pedagogy of freedom: Ethics, democracy, and civic courage*. Lanham, MD: Rowman and Littlefield.

Freire, P. (1998b). *Pedagogy of the heart*. New York: Continuum.

Freire, P. (1997). "A response". In P. Freire, J. W. Fraser, D. Macedo, T. McKinnon, and W. T. Stokes, eds. *Mentoring the mentor: A critical dialogue with Paulo Freire*. New York: Peter Lang, 303–29.

Freire, P. (1995). "Reply to discussants". In M. de Figueiredo-Cowen and D. Gastaldo, *Paulo Freire at the Institute*. The Brazilian Educators Lecture Series, Institute of Education. London: University of London.

Freire, P. (1994a). *Pedagogy of hope: Reliving pedagogy of the oppressed*. R. R. Barr, trans. New York: Continuum.

Freire, P. (1994b). *Education for critical consciousness*. New York: Continuum.

Freire, P. (1990). *Pedagogy of the oppressed*. New York: Continuum.

Freire, P. (1985). *The politics of education: Culture, power, and liberation*. New York: Bergin and Garvey.

Freire, P., and Macedo, D. P. (1995). "A dialogue: Culture, language, and race". *Harvard Educational Review* 65(3), 377–402.

Fromm, E. (2006). *The art of loving* (fiftieth anniversary edition). New York: Harper Perennial Modern Classics.

Fullan, M. (2006). *Turnaround leadership*. San Francisco, CA: Jossey-Bass.

Fullan, M. (2001). *Leading in a culture of change*. San Francisco, CA: Jossey-Bass.

Gardner, H. (2000). *The disciplined mind*. New York: Penguin Books.

Gardner, H. (1983). *Frames of mind: The theory of multiple intelligences*. New York: Basic Books.

Gay, G. (2005). "Foreword: Making better sense of multicultural education: Principles to practice". In R. H. Sheets, *Diversity pedagogy: Examining the role of culture in the teaching-learning process*. Boston: Pearson Education, xv–xix.

Giles, D., Smythe, E., and Spence, D. (2012). "Exploring relationships in education: A phenomenological inquiry". *Australian Journal of Adult Learning* 52(2), 214–36.

Gilroy, M. (2006). "Jaime Escalante still stands and delivers: A 30-year overnight success". *The Hispanic Outlook in Higher Education* 16(35). Retrieved from http://ez-

proxy.selu.edu/login?url=http://search.proquest.com/docview/219180518?accountid=13772.
Ginott, H. (1972). *Teacher and child*. New York: Macmillan.
Giroux, H. A. (2011). *On critical pedagogy*. New York: Continuum.
Giroux, H. A. (2007). "Introduction: Democracy, education, and the politics of critical pedagogy". In P. McLaren and J. L. Kincheloe, *Critical pedagogy: Where are we now?* . New York: Peter Lang, 1–5.
Giroux, H. A. (1988). *Teachers as intellectuals: Towards a critical pedagogy of learning*. South Hadley, MA: Bergin and Garvey Publishers.
Gollnick, D. M., and Chinn, P. C. (2013). *Multicultural education in a pluralistic society* (ninth edition). Boston: Pearson Education.
Graves, D. H. (2001). *The energy to teach*. Portsmouth, NH: Heinemann.
Guillaume, A. M. (2004). *K–12 classroom teaching: A primer for new professionals* (second edition). Upper Saddle River, NJ: Pearson Education.
Gutiérrez, G. (1993). *Las Casas: In search of the poor of Jesus Christ*. R. Barr, trans. Maryknoll, NY: Orbis Books.
Gutiérrez, G. (1990). *The truth shall make you free* M. O'Connell, trans. Maryknoll, NY: Orbis Books.
Hammerness, K., Darling-Hammond, L., Bransford, J., Berliner, D., Cochran-Smith, M., McDonald, M., and Zeichner, K. (2005). "How teachers learn and develop". In L. Darling-Hammond and J. Bransford, eds. *Preparing teachers for a changing world: What teachers should learn and be able to do*. San Francisco, CA: Jossey-Bass, 358–89.
Hancock, L. (2005). "How are the kids?" *Columbia Journalism Review* 43(6), 22–28. Retrieved from http://ezproxy.selu.edu/login?url=http://search.proquest.com/docview/230376142?accountid=13772.
Hargreaves, A. (2001). "Emotional geographies of teaching". *Teachers College Record* 103(6), 1056–80.
Hargreaves, A., and Shirley, D. (2009). *The fourth way: The inspiring future of educational change*. Thousand Oaks, CA: Corwin Press.
Harrison, C., and Killion, J. (2007). "Ten roles for teacher leaders". *Educational Leadership* 65(1), 74–77.
Hart, T. (2000). "Inspiration as transpersonal knowing". In T. Hart, P. L. Nelson, and K. Puhakka, eds. *Transpersonal knowing: Exploring the horizon of consciousness*. Albany, NY: State University of New York Press, 31–53.
Hart, T. (1998). "Inspiration: exploring the experience and its meaning". *Journal of Humanistic Psychology* 38(7), 7–35.
Henderson, J. G., and Hawthorne, R. D. (2000). *Transforming curriculum leadership* (second edition). Upper Saddle, NJ: Merrill.
Henry, J. (1991). "Making sense of creativity". In J. Henry, ed. *Creative management*. Newbury Park, CA: Sage Publications, 3–11.
Hoffman, D., and Levak, B. A. (2003). "Personalizing schools". *Educational Leadership* 61(1), 30–34. Retrieved from http://ezproxy.selu.edu/login?url=http://search.proquest.com/docview/224842868?accountid=13772.
Horowitz, S. S. (2012). "The science and art of listening". *Sunday Review, New York Times*. Retrieved from http://www.nytimes.com/2012/11/11/opinion/sunday/why-listening-is-so-much-more-than-hearing.html?_r=0.
Inglis, W. B. (1959). "Personalism, analysis, and education". *International Review of Education* 5(4), 383–99.
Jacobs, G. (2012). "Relationships: The heart of early childhood education". *YC Young Children* 67(5), 6–7, 53. Retrieved from http://ezproxy.selu.edu/login?url=http://search.proquest.com/docview/1439084884?accountid=13772.
Janesick, V. J. (2001). *The assessment debate: A reference handbook*. Santa Barbara, CA: ABC-CLIO.
Jezreel, J. (1997). "Why the preferential option for the poor is not optional". *U.S. Catholic* 62(11), 30–35.

Johnson, C. (2001). "The elusive art of 'mindfulness'". *The Chronicle of Higher Education* 47(31), B10–B12. Retrieved from http://ezproxy.selu.edu/login?url=http://search.proquest.com/docview/214703176?accountid=13772.

Johnson, S. M., and Donaldson, M. L. (2007). "Overcoming the obstacles to leadership". *Educational Leadership* 65(1), 8–13.

Johnson, T. W., and Reed, R. F. (2008). *Philosophical documents in education* (third edition). Boston: Pearson Education.

Katz, L. G. (1993a). *Dispositions: Definitions and implications for early childhood practices.* Catalog No. 211 Perspectives from ERIC/EECE: A Monograph Series, No. 4. Urbana, IL: ERIC Clearinghouse on Elementary and Early Childhood Education. Retrieved from http://ceep.crc.uiuc.edu/eecearchive/books/disposit.html.

Katz, L. G. (1993b). *Dispositions as educational goals.* ERIC: ED363454. Urbana, IL: ERIC Clearinghouse on Elementary and Early Childhood Education. Retrieved from http://ceep.crc.uiuc.edu/eecearchive/digests/1993/katzdi93.html.

Katzenmeyer, M., and Moller, G. (2009). *Awakening the sleeping giant: Helping teachers develop as leaders* (third edition). Thousand Oaks, CA: Corwin Press.

Katzenmeyer, M., and Moller, G. (2001). *Awakening the sleeping giant: Leadership development for teachers* (second edition). Thousand Oaks, CA: Corwin Press.

Kauchak, D., and Eggen, P. (2005). Introduction to teaching: Becoming a professional. University of Phoenix Custom Edition e-Text: Prentice-Hall/Merrill. Retrieved August 12, 2007, from University of Phoenix, rEsource, AED Teaching as a Profession website.

Kersey, K. C. and Masterson, M. L. (2009). "Teachers connecting with families: In the best interest of children". *YC Young Children* 64(5), 34-38. Retrieved from http://ezproxy.selu.edu/login?url=http://search.proquest.com/docview/197609274?accountid=13772.

Khalifa, M., Arnold, N. W., and Newcomb, W. (2015). "Understand and advocate for communites first". *Phi Delta Kappan* 96(7), 21–25.

Kincheloe, J. L. (2008). *Critical pedagogy* (second edition). New York: Peter Lang.

Kincheloe, J. L. (2006). "A critical complex epistemology of practice". *Taboo*, 10(2), 85–98.

Kincheloe, J. L. (1992). *Liberation theology and the attempt to establish an emancipatory system of meaning.* Paper presented at the Bergamo Conference on Curriculum Theory and Classroom Practice, Dayton, OH. In W. Pinar, W. Reynolds, P. Slattery, and P. Taubman, *Understanding curriculum.* New York: Peter Lang, 606–60.

Kincheloe, J. L., Slattery, P., and Steinberg, S. R. (2000). *Contextualizing teaching: Introduction to education and educational foundations.* New York: Addison Wesley Longman.

Kirylo, J. D. (2011). *Paulo Freire: The man from Recife.* New York: Peter Lang.

Kirylo, J. D. (2009). "No more theories please! A guide for elementary teachers by L.K. Masao" (book review). *Childhood Education* 86(1), 58.

Kirylo, J. D. (2008). "Ten essential practices and attitudes: A guide for school teachers". Olney, MD: Association for Childhood Education International. Retrieved from http://www.acei.org/tenessentials.pdf.

Kirylo, J. (2006). "Preferential option for the poor: Making a pedagogical choice". *Childhood Education* 82(5), 266–70.

Kirylo, J. D. (2001). "A historical overview of liberation theology: Some implications for the Christian educator". *Journal of Research on Christian Education* 10(1), 53–86.

Kirylo, J. D., and Nauman, A. (2006). "The depersonalization of education and the language of accountability: A view from a local newspaper". *Journal of Curriculum and Pedagogy* 3(1), 187–206.

Klem, A. M., and Connell, J. P. (2004). "Relationships matter: Linking teacher support to student engagement and achievement". *The Journal of School Health* 74(7), 262–73. Retrieved from http://ezproxy.selu.edu/login?url=http://search.proquest.com/docview/215675398?accountid=13772.

Koch, J. (2009). *So you want to be a teacher? Teaching and learning in the 21st century*. Boston: Houghton Mifflin Company.
Kohn, A. (2010). "Turning children into data: A skeptic's guide to assessment programs". *Education Week* Retrieved from http://www.edweek.org/ew/articles/2010/08/25/01kohn_ep.h30.html?tkn=WMVFLa0LfemilvpFh/WxiJkx+P2bTGNrKTAv.
Kohn, A. (2000). *The case against standardized testing: Raising the scores, ruining the schools*. Portsmouth, NH: Heinemann.
Kohn, A. (1999). *Punished by rewards: The trouble with gold stars, incentive plans, A's, praise, and other bribes*. Boston: Houghton Mifflin Company.
Komonchak, J. A., Collins, M., and Lane, D. A., eds. (1987). *The new dictionary of theology*. Collegeville, MN: The Liturgical Press.
Kopkowski, C. (2008). "Why they leave: Lack of respect, NCLB, and underfunding—In a topsy-turvy profession, what can make today's teachers stay?" Retrieved from http://www.nea.org/home/12630.htm.
Kozol, J. (2005). *The shame of the nation: The restoration of apartheid schooling in America*. New York: Three Rivers Press.
Kozol, J. (1995). "A weary crusader". *The Dallas Morning News*, 4C.
LaBoskey, V. K. (1994). *Development of reflective practice: A study of preservice teachers*. New York: Teachers College Press.
LaCaze, D., and Kirylo, J. (2012). "A practical guide to a principled classroom". *Focus on Teacher Education: A Quarterly ACEI Publication for the Education Community* 11(3), 8–9.
Lagemann, E. C. (2000). *An elusive science: The troubling history of education research*. Chicago, IL: The University of Chicago Press.
Lakoff, G. (2004). *Don't think of an elephant: Know your values and frame the debate*. White River Junction, VT: Chelsea Green.
Leithwood, K.A., and Poplin, M. S. (1992). The move toward transformational leadership. *Educational Leadership* 49(5), 8–12.
Lewis, D., and Weigert, A. (1985). Trust as a social reality. *Social Forces* 63(4), 967–85.
Lewis, M. (2008). *Leadership practices that build trust: A closer look at trust and its importance in the principal-teacher relationship* (unpublished doctoral dissertation). Toronto: University of Toronto Press.
Lieberman, A., and Friedrich, L. (2007). Teachers, writers, leaders. *Educational Leadership* 65(1), 42–47.
Lincoln, Y. S., and Guba, E. G. (1980). "The distinction between merit and worth in evaluation". *Educational Evaluation and Policy Analysis* 2(4), 61–71.
Locke, J. (1690). *An essay concerning human understanding*. The University of Adelaide Library, Australia. Retrieved from ebooks.adelaide.edu.au/l/locke/john/l81u/.
Loewen, J. W. (2010). *Teaching what really happened: How to avoid the tyranny of textbooks and get students excited about doing history*. New York: Teachers College Press.
Loewen, J. W. (2007). *Lies my teacher told me: Everything your American history textbook got wrong*. New York: Touchstone.
Longstreet, W., and Shane, H. G. (1993). *Curriculum for a new millennium*. Boston: Allyn and Bacon.
Lore, D. C. (2014). "Parents asked to pay for test prep workbooks, fueling common core frustration". *Staten Island Advance*. Retrieved from http://www.silive.com/news/index.ssf/2014/10/common_core_sending_out_mixed.html.
Lovewell, K. (2012). *Every teacher matters*. St. Albans, UK: Ecademy Press.
Manvell, E. C. (2009). *Teaching is a privilege: Twelve essential understandings for beginning teachers*. Lanham, MD: Rowman and Littlefield Education.
Marsh, C. J., and Willis, G. (2007). *Curriculum: Alternative approaches, ongoing issues* (fourth edition). Upper Saddle River, NJ: Pearson Education.
Marshall, J. M. (2009). "Describing the elephant: Preservice teachers talk about spiritual reasons for becoming a teacher". *Teacher Education Quarterly*, 36(2), 25–44.
Marzano, R. J. (2000). *Transforming classroom grading*. Alexandria, VA: Association for Supervision and Curriculum Development.

Masao, L. K. (2009). *No more theories please! A guide for elementary teachers*. Lanham, MD: Rowman and Littlefield Education.

Matthews, J. (2006). "Just whose idea was all this testing?" *The Washington Post*. Retrieved from http://www.washingtonpost.com/wp-dyn/content/article/2006/11/13/AR2006111301007.html

Mathews, J. (1989). *Escalante: The best teacher in America*. New York: Henry Holt and Co.

Maxwell, J. C. (n.d.). *Leadership is influence: Nothing more, nothing less*. Retrieved from http://www.buildingchurchleaders.com/articles/2005/090905.html?start=1.

May, R. (1975). *The courage to create*. New York: W. W. Norton and Company.

Mayeroff, M. (1971). *On caring*. New York: Harper and Row.

McAleer, N. (1991). "The roots of inspiration". In J. Henry, ed. *Creative Management*. Newbury Park, CA: Sage Publications, 12–15.

Merideth, E. M. (2007). *Leadership strategies for teachers* (second edition). Thousand Oaks, CA: Corwin Press.

Merriam-Webster's collegiate dictionary (eleventh edition). (2012). Springfield, MA: Merriam-Webster.

Mitra, D. L. (2003). "Student voice in school reform: Reframing student-teacher relationships". *McGill Journal of Education* 38(2), 289–304. Retrieved from http://ezproxy.selu.edu/login?url=http://search.proquest.com/docview/202720547?accountid=13772.

Moore, K. A., Redd, Z., Burkhauser, M., Mbwana, K., and Collins, A. (2009). "Children in poverty: Trends, consequences, and policy options". *Child Trends Research Brief*. Retrieved from www.childtrends.org.

Mother Teresa (1996). *Mother Teresa: In my own words*. Compiled by Jose-Luis Gonzalez Baldo. Gramercy Books: New York.

Mother Teresa. (1983). *Words to love by . . .* Notre Dame, IN: Ave Maria Press.

Mueller, J. (2014) *Portfolios*. Authentic Assessment Toolbox. Retrieved from http://jfmueller.faculty.noctrl.edu/toolbox/portfolios.htm.

Murphy, J. (2005). *Connecting teacher leadership and school improvement*. Thousand Oaks, CA: Corwin Press.

NAEYC (2009). "Developmentally appropriate practice in early childhood programs serving children from birth through age 8". Retrieved from https://www.naeyc.org/files/naeyc/file/positions/PSDAP.pdf.

National Center for Education Statistics (n.d.). *Children and youth with disabilities*. U.S. Department of Education Institute of Education Sciences. Retrieved from https://nces.ed.gov/programs/coe/indicator_cgg.asp.

National Conference of Catholic Bishops. (1995). *A decade after economic justice for all: Continuing principles, changing context, new challenges*. Washington, DC: United States Catholic Conference.

National Conference of Catholic Bishops. (1994). *Communities of salt and light: Reflections on the social mission of the parish*. Washington, DC: United States Catholic Conference.

National Conference of Catholic Bishops. (1986). *Economic justice for all: Pastoral letter on Catholic social teaching and the U.S. economy*. Washington, DC: United States Catholic Conference.

National Council of Teachers of English (NCTE) (2013). *Formative assessment that truly informs instruction*. Retrieved from http://www.ncte.org/library/NCTEFiles/Resources/Positions/formative-assessment_single.pdf.

Nelson, H. (2013). *Testing more, teaching less: What America's obsession with student testing costs in money and lost instructional time* . American Federation of Teachers (AFL-CIO). Retrieved from http://www.aft.org/sites/default/files/news/testingmore2013.pdf.

Niebuhr, R. (1927). *Does civilization need religion?* New York: Macmillan.

Nielsen, K. E. (2010). *Beyond the miracle worker: The remarkable life of Anne Sullivan Macy and her extraordinary friendship with Helen Keller*. Boston: Beacon Press.

Noddings, N. (2013). *Caring: A relational approach to ethics and moral education* (second edition, updated). Berkeley and Los Angeles, CA: University of California Press.

Noddings, N. (1992). *The challenge to care in schools: An alternative approach to education*. New York: Teachers College Press.

Nouwen, H. (1996). *Can you drink the cup?* Notre Dame, IN: Ave Maria Press.

Nouwen, H. J. M. (1983). *Gracias: A Latin American journal*. Maryknoll, NY: Orbis Books.

Ozmon, H., and Craver, S. (1990). *Philosophical foundations of education* (fourth edition). Columbus, OH: Merrill Publishing Company.

Pai, Y., and Adler, S. A. (2001). *Cultural foundations of education* (third edition). Upper Saddle River, NJ: Merrill Prentice Hall.

Palmer, P. J. (2007). *The courage to teach*. San Francisco, CA: Jossey-Bass.

Palmer, P. (1993). *To know as we are known: Education as a spiritual journey*. New York: HarperSanFrancisco.

Parankimalil, J. (2012). *Meaning, nature and scope of educational psychology*. Retrieved from http://johnparankimalil.wordpress.com/2012/03/09/meaning-nature-and-scope-of- educational-psychology/.

Parkay, F. W., and Hass, G. (2000). *Curriculum planning: A contemporary approach* (seventh edition). Boston: Allyn and Bacon.

Perrone, V. (1991). "On standardized testing". *Childhood Education* 67(3), 132–42.

Perrone, V. (1977). *The abuses of standardized testing*. Bloomington, IN: The Phi Delta Kappa Educational Foundation.

Piaget, J. (1959). *Language and thought of the child*. M. Grabain, trans. New York: Humanities Press.

Piaget, J. (1952). *Origins of intelligence in children*. New York: International Universities Press.

Pinar, W. (1994). *Autobiography, politics, and sexuality: Essays in curriculum theory, 1972–1992*. Dubuque, IA: Kendall/Hunt.

Pinar, W., and Grumet, M. R. (1976). *Toward a poor curriculum*. Dubuque, IA: Kendall/Hunt.

Pinar, W., Reynolds, W., Slattery, P., and Taubman, P. (1995). *Understanding curriculum*. New York: Peter Lang.

Player, M. (2000). "Portfolio assessment: Taking charge of learning. *Teach*, 15. Retrieved from http://ezproxy.selu.edu/login?url=http://search.proquest.com/docview/214499695?accountid=13772.

Ponton, R. F. (2012). "Mindfulness and mastery in counseling: Introduction to the special issue". *Journal of Mental Health Counseling* 34(3), 189–96. Retrieved from http://ezproxy.selu.edu/login?url=http://search.proquest.com/docview/1027919895?accountid=13772.

Popham, J. W. (2008). *Transformative assessment*. Alexandria, VA: Association for Supervision and Curriculum Development.

Pugach, M.C. (2006). *Because teaching matters*. Hoboken, NJ: John Wiley and Sons.

Purpel, D. (1989). *The moral and spiritual crisis in education: A curriculum for justice and compassion in education*. New York: Bergin and Garvey.

Quinn, S., and Owen, S. (2014). "Freedom to grow: Children's perspective of student voice". *Childhood Education* 90(3), 192–201.

Ravitch, D. (2013). *Reign of error: The hoax of the privatization movement and the danger to America's public schools*. New York: Alfred A. Knopf.

Ravitch, D. (2010). "Ravitch to Obama: 'Change course before it is too late'". *The Washington Post*, interview with Valerie Strauss. Retrieved from http://voices.washingtonpost.com/answer-sheet/diane-ravitch/ravitch-to-obama-change-course.html#more.

Reeves, D. (2007). "Teachers step up". *Educational Leadership* 65(1), 87–88.

Ribot, T. A. (1973). *Essay on the creative imagination*. New York: Arno Press.

Richardson, V., and Fallona, C. (2001). "Classroom management as method and manner". *Journal of Curriculum Studies* 33(6), 705–28.

Ritchhart, R., and Perkins, D. N. (2000). "Life in the mindful classroom: Nurturing the disposition of mindfulness". *Journal of Social Issues* 56(1), 27–47.
Roberts, P. (2010). *Paulo Freire in the 21st century*. Boulder, CO: Paradigm Publishers.
Roberts, P. (2000). *Education, literacy, and humanization: Exploring the work of Paulo Freire*. Westport, CT: Bergin and Garvey.
Robinson, K. (2009a). "Reach for Michelin stars, not McSchools". *The Times Educational Supplement* (4844), 33. Retrieved from http://ezproxy.selu.edu/login?url=http://search.proquest.com/docview/209469525?accountid=13772.
Robinson, K. (2009b). In A. M. Azzam, "Why creativity now? A conversation with Sir Ken Robinson". *Educational Leadership* 67(1), 22–26. Retrieved from http://www.ascd.org/publications/educational-leadership/sept09/vol67/num01/Why-Creativity-Now%C2%A2-A-Conversation-with-Sir-Ken-Robinson.aspx.
Robinson, K. (n.d.). *TED Talks Education*. Retrieved from http://sirkenrobinson.com/?s=educationandpaged=2.
Rodgers, C. (2002). "Defining reflection: Another look at John Dewey and reflective thinking". *Teachers College Record* 104(4), 842–66.
Rohr, R. (2011). *Falling upward: A spirituality for the two halves of life*. San Francisco, CA: Jossey-Bass.
Rose, M. (1989). *Lives on the boundary*. New York: Penguin Books.
Rousseau, J. J. (1921). *Emile, or education* Barbara Foxley, trans. London and Toronto: J. M. Dent and Sons; New York: E. P. Dutton. Retrieved from http://lf-oll.s3.amazonaws.com/titles/2256/Rousseau_1499_EBk_v6.0.pdf.
Rousseau, J.J. (1762). *Emile*. In S. M. Cahn (1970), *The philosophical foundations of education*. New York: Harper and Row, 155–76.
Ryan, K., and Cooper, J. M. (2013). *Those who can, teach* (thirteenth edition). Belmont, CA: Wadsworth, Cengage Learning.
Ryan, M. (2008). *Ask the teacher: A practitioner's guide to teaching and learning in the diverse classroom* (second edition). Boston: Pearson Education.
Sacks, P. (1999). *Standardized minds*. Cambridge, MA: Perseus Publishing.
Sahlberg, P. (2011). *Finnish Lessons: What can the world learn from educational change in Finland*. New York: Teachers College Press.
Sanborn, M. (2006). *You don't need a title to be a leader*. Colorado Springs, CO: Waterbrook Press.
Santrock, J. W. (2009). *Educational psychology*. New York: McGraw-Hill.
Schön, D.A. (1987). *Educating the reflective practitioner*. San Francisco, CA: Jossey-Bass Publishers.
Schön, D.A. (1983). *The reflective practitioner: How professionals think in action*. New York: Basic Books.
Schussler, D. L., Stooksberry, L. M., and Bercaw, L. A. (2010). "Understanding teacher candidate dispositions: Reflecting to build self-awareness". *Journal of Teacher Education* 61(4), 350–63.
Shor, I., and Freire, P. (1987). *A pedagogy for liberation: Dialogues on transforming education*. New York: Bergin and Garvey.
Shulman, D. (2008). "Illumination, imagination, creativity: Rājaśekhara, Kuntaka, and Jagannātha on Pratibhā". *Journal of Indian Philosophy* 36(4), 481–505.
Siegel, D. J. (2013). "Foreword". In L. Cozolino, *The social neuroscience of education: Optimizing attachment and learning in the classroom*. New York: W. W. Norton and Company, xi–xiv.
Siegel, D. J. (2001). "Toward an interpersonal neurobiology of the developing mind: Attachment relationships, "mindsight," and neural integration". *Infant Mental Health Journal* 22(1–2), 67–94.
Siegel, D. J. (1999). *The developing mind: How relationships and the brain interact to shape who we are*. New York: The Guilford Press.
Siegel, D. (n.d.) "What is mindsight? An interview with Dr. Dan Siegel". Retrieved from http://www.psychalive.org/what-is-mindsight-an-interview-with-dr-dan-siegel/.

Siegel, D. J., and Hartzell, M. (2003). *Parenting from the inside out: How a deeper self-understanding can help you raise children who thrive*. New York: Jeremy P. Tarcher/Putnam.
Sizer, T. R., and Sizer, N. F. (1999). *The students are watching*. Boston: Beacon Press.
Slattery, P. (1995). *Curriculum development in the postmodern era*. New York: Garland Publishing.
Slattery, P., and Rapp, D. (2003). *Ethics and the foundation of education: Teaching convictions in a postmodern world*. Boston: Allyn and Bacon.
Slavin, R. E. (2000). *Educational psychology: Theory and practice* (sixth edition). Boston: Allyn and Bacon.
Solley, B. A. (2007). "On standardized testing: An ACEI position paper". *Childhood Education* 84(1), 31–37.
Sparks-Langer, G. M., and Colton, A. B. (1991). "Synthesis of research on teachers' reflective thinking". *Educational Leadership* 48(6), 37–43.
Spilt, J. L., Koomen, H. M. Y., and Thijs, J. T. (2011). "Teacher wellbeing: The importance of teacher-student relationships". *Educational Psychology Review* 23(4), 457–77. Retrieved from doi:http://dx.doi.org/10.1007/s10648-011-9170-y.
Strauss, V. (2013). "How much time do school districts spend on standardized testing? This much". *The Washington Post*. Retrieved from http://www.washingtonpost.com/blogs/answer-sheet/wp/2013/07/25/how-much-time-do-school-districts-spend-on-standardized-testing-this-much/.
Sullo, R. A. (1999). *The inspiring teacher: New beginnings for the 21st century*. Annapolis Junction, MD: National Education Association Professional Library.
Thorndike, E. L. (1918). "The nature, purposes, and general methods of measurement of educational products". In G. M. Whipple, ed. *The seventeenth yearbook of the national society for the study of education: The measurement of educational products* (part 2). Bloomington, IL: Public School Publishing Co., 16–24.
Thrash, T. M., and Elliot, A. J. (2004). "Inspiration: Core characteristics, component processes, antecedents, and function". *Journal of Personality and Social Psychology* 87(6), 957–73.
Thrash, T. M., and Elliot, A. J. (2003). "Inspiration as a psychological construct". *Journal of Personality and Social Psychology* 84(4), 871–89.
Tomlinson, C. A. (2014). *The differentiated classroom: Responding to the needs of all learners* (second edition). Alexandria, VA: ASCD.
Tomlinson, C. A. (2013). *Defensible differentiation: Why, what, and how*. London: American School in London Learning Institute. Retrieved from http://www.caroltomlinson.com/Presentations/Tomlinson%20ASL%20Institute%206-13%20V2.pdf.
Tyler, R. (1949). *Basic principles of curriculum and instruction*. Chicago, IL: University of Chicago Press.
U.S. Census Bureau (2014). "Poverty Main". *United States Census Bureau*. Retrieved from https://www.census.gov/hhes/www/poverty/.
U.S. Congress, Office of Technology Assessment (1992). *Testing in American schools: Asking the right questions*, OTA-SET-519. Washington, DC: U.S. Government Printing Office. Retrieved from http://files.eric.ed.gov/fulltext/ED340770.pdf.
United States National Commission on Excellence in Education. (1983). *A nation at risk: The imperative for educational reform: A report to the Nation and the Secretary of Education, United States Department of Education*. Washington, DC. Retrieved from http://www2.ed.gov/pubs/NatAtRisk/index.html.
Vygotsky, L. (1978). *Mind in society: The development of higher psychological processes*. M. Cole, V. John-Steiner, S. Scribner, and E. Souberman, eds. Cambridge, MA: Harvard University Press.
Vygotsky, L. (1962). *Thought and language*. Cambridge, MA: MIT Press.
Walker, J. E., Shea, T. M., and Bauer, A. M. (2007). *Behavior management: A practical approach for educators* (ninth edition). Columbus, OH: Allyn and Bacon/Merrill.
Ward, W. A. (1970). *Fountains of faith*. Anderson, SC: Droke House Publishers.

Ward, W. A. (1968). *Thoughts of a Christian optimist*. Anderson, SC: Droke House Publishers.
Wasley, P. A. (1991). *Teachers who lead: The rhetoric of reform and the realities of practice*. New York: Columbia University Press.
Watson, J. B. (1970). *Behaviorism*. (first published in 1924). New York: W. W. Norton and Company.
Wawrytko, S. A. (1982). "Confucius and Kant: The ethics of respect". *Philosophy East and West* 32(3), 237–57.
Webb, L. D., Metha, A., and Jordan, K. F. (2007). *Foundations of American education* (fifth edition). Upper Saddle River, NJ: Pearson Education
Weber, L. R., and Carter, A. (1998). "On constructing trust: Temporality, self-disclosure, and perspective taking". *The International Journal of Sociology and Social Policy* 18(1), 7–26.
Weeks-Channel, S. (2010). "Inspiring to greatness". *Making Connections* 12(1), 1–3.
Wellington, B. (1991). "The promise of reflective practice". *Educational Leadership* 48(6), 4–5.
Wheatley, K. F. (n.d.). *Teacher persistence: A crucial disposition, with implications for teacher education*. Retrieved from http://www.usca.edu/essays/vol32002/wheatley.pdf.
Wheeler, J., and Richey, D. (2009). *Behavior management: Principles and practices of positive behavior supports* (second edition). Upper Saddle River, NJ: Prentice Hall.
Whitaker, T. (2004). *What great teachers do differently: 14 things that matter most*. Larchmont: NY: Eye on Education.
Wiggins, G. (2012). "Seven keys to effective feedback". *Educational Leadership* 70(1), 10–16. Retrieved from http://www.ascd.org/publications/educational-leadership/sept12/vol70/num01/Seven-Keys-to-Effective-Feedback.aspx.
Wiggins, G. (2011). *Formative vs summative assessment—And unthinking policy about them*. Retrieved from http://grantwiggins.wordpress.com/2011/08/25/formative-vs-summative-assessment-and-unthinking-policy-about-them/.
Wiggins, G. (1998). *Educative assessment: Designing assessments to inform and improve student performance*. San Francisco, CA: Jossey-Bass.
Wiggins, G. P. (1993). *Assessing student performance: Exploring the purpose and limits of testing*. San Francisco, CA: Jossey-Bass.
Witmer, M.M. (2005). "The fourth R in education-relationships". *The Clearing House* 78(5), 224–28. Retrieved from http://ezproxy.selu.edu/login?url=http://search.proquest.com/docview/196863180?accountid=13772.
Woo, J. G. (2012). "Buber from the Cartesian perspective? A critical review of reading Buber's pedagogy". *Studies in Philosophy and Education* 31(6), 569–85.
Wormeli, R. (2005). "Busting myths about differentiated instruction". *Principal Leadership* 5(7), 28–33. Retrieved from http://ezproxy.selu.edu/login?url=http://search.proquest.com/docview/234990154?accountid=13772.
Wynne, J. (2001). "Teachers as leaders in education reform". ERIC Clearinghouse on Teaching and Teacher Education. Washington, DC. Retrieved from http://files.eric.ed.gov/fulltext/ED462376.pdf.

Index

accommodation, 90
achievement gap, 157–158
Aldridge, Jerry, 87
America 2000, 124
assessment, x, xiv, 27, 69, 77, 113–120, 121n6, 124, 126n2, 129–142, 142n1, 145; formative, 138, 142; portfolio, 114, 135, 137, 140–142, 142n2; summative, 141, 142n1. *See also* tests

assimilation, 90
attitude, 13–14, 26, 28, 48, 54, 56, 65, 101, 127n6, 146
autobiographical, x, xiii, 68, 98, 165
axiology, 10
Ayers, William, 18, 37

Bacon, Francis, 83, 86n1
Bandura, Albert, 88, 106
Banks, Amy, 31, 33, 157
Banks, James A., 53, 55–56
Barone, Thomas, 26; Barth, Roland S., 50
Baryshnikov, Mikhail, 73
behavior management, 78–79, 80n2, 103
behavioral theory, 105
behaviorism, 85–89, 93n1, 105
belief, 18–19, 22, 23n1, 25, 56, 65, 83, 87–88, 97, 162
Binet-Simon, 120
Blight, David W., 55
Boff, Clodovis, 154
Boff, Leonardo, 154
Boone, Herman, 62, 64–67
brain, 31–34, 34n1, 36, 41, 90, 100, 109n2, 163
Buber, Martin, 36

care, 18, 20–21, 47, 51, 51n1, 88, 91, 138, 159
child development, 77, 86n2, 87, 101
Chomsky, Noam, 93n2, 129
classroom management, 78, 80n1, 97, 100–101, 104
cognitive learning theory, 106
cognitivism, 86–87, 89
Comenius, John Amos, 82–84
Comer, James, 35, 101, 159
Common Core State Standards (CCSS), 129–130, 135n1, 146
Cozolino, Louis, 33
common school, 118
community, x, 5n1, 7, 16–19, 25, 34–35, 40, 45, 50–51, 63–65, 69, 125, 149, 152, 154, 155n1, 157–159
compassion, 17, 20–22, 45, 74
connoisseur, 72–74
consciousness, 3, 64, 88, 162–163
consistency, 21, 43–44, 86n1, 102, 118
constructivism, 99, 104n1, 107
Cozolino, Louis, 33
Crain, William, 82–85, 86n2, 88–89, 91, 93n1–93n2, 104n2
creativity, 14, 69, 71–72, 160n1, 162–163
credibility, 4, 149
critical pedagogy, x, 153–154, 165
Csikszentmihalyi, Mihaly, 163
Cummins, Jim, 55
currere, 68, 165
curriculum, xiv–xv, 57, 63–64, 68–69, 77–79, 100–101, 115, 119, 123–124, 130–131, 135n1, 138–141, 146–147, 149, 160n1, 165

Danielson, Charlotte, 140–141, 146–149
Darder, Antonia, 154
Darling-Hammond, Linda, 5, 26, 109, 117, 130–131, 135n3

deductive (reasoning), 86n1
Delpit, Lisa, 55–56, 157
developmentally appropriate practice, xiii, 8, 16, 22, 27, 69, 100–101, 133, 142n2, 152, 159
Dewey, John, 13–16, 25, 54, 117–118, 120, 125, 142, 145, 148, 157
dialogue, 8, 17, 20, 36–37, 39–42, 43, 49, 118, 152
discipline, xiii, 26, 70, 101, 104, 108, 140, 162
disequilibrium, 90
disposition, xiii, 10, 13–16, 17–19, 22, 26, 36, 45, 48, 54, 68, 102, 108–109, 123, 149
diversity, xv, 4, 15, 49, 53–54, 56–57, 152

Eggen, Paul, 3, 41, 77, 79, 90–92, 108
Eisner, Eliot, 71–73, 79
Elementary and Secondary Act (ESEA), 124
Elkind, David, 77
Elliot, Andrew J., 61, 162–163
enthusiasm, 13, 16, 62, 108, 149, 162
epistemology, 9
equality, 15, 57, 65
Escalante, Jaime, 62–67
evaluation, 41, 45, 113–115, 123, 129, 135n3, 159
expectation, 4, 15, 65

faith, 17, 18, 22, 27, 40, 61, 85, 154, 155n1, 162
Flinders, David J., 74
Freedom Writers, 64
Freire, Paulo, 9, 10, 18–20, 36–37, 39–40, 55–56, 104n1, 152, 155n2
Fromm, Erich, 17
Fullan, Michael, 50, 149

Galton, Francis, 119, 121n3
Gardner, Howard, 69, 107
Ginott, Haim G., 68, 92
Giroux, Henry, 150, 154, 165
Goals 2000, 124, 127n4
Graves, Donald H., 132
Gruwell, Erin, 62–67
Guba, Egon G., 114–115

Gutiérrez, Gustavo, 37, 55

habit, 13–14, 27, 54
Hargreaves, Andy, 49, 149
Hart, Tobin, 61–62, 68, 161–163
Hartzell, Mary, 37–38, 47–48
Hass, Glen J., xiii, 81, 87–88, 105–106
hope, 4, 17–19, 21–22, 27, 40, 47, 57, 64–65, 67, 74, 103, 147, 150, 154
humanism, 86–87, 92
humanization, 9
humility, 17, 19–22, 23n1, 40

inductive (reasoning), 86n1
inspiration, xiv, 26, 61–63, 67–70, 74, 161–163
instruction: deductive, 98–100; differentiated, 80n2, 100; inductive, 98–100, 106; integrated, 98, 100, 140
integrity, xiii, 5, 42–43, 46, 50–51, 91, 149
Intelligence Quotient (IQ), 119–120, 121n5

Janesick, Valerie J., 117, 120, 123–124, 141
joy, 5, 67, 133, 167
Jung, Carl, 20
justice, 5, 15, 43, 57, 65
Jung, Carl, 20

Katz, Lilian G., 14
Katzenmeyer, Marilyn H., 145–146, 149
Kauchak, Don, 3, 41, 77, 79, 90–92, 108
Kincheloe, Joe, ix, 8–9, 104n1, 154
King, Jr., Martin Luther, 73
Kirylo, James D., 10, 15, 21
Kohn, Alfie, 106, 123, 125–126, 129
Kozol, Jonathan, 131, 153

Lagemann, Ellen C., 117–120, 121n1
Lakoff, George, 158
leader, 82, 92, 145–146; teacher-leader, x, 27, 147–149, 153, 154
leadership, 49–50, 65, 121n1, 145–149; teacher leadership, 146–150
Lincoln, Yvonna S., 114–115
listen, 3, 15, 19, 39–41, 43–44, 51n1, 152
Locke, John, 83–85, 86n2

Loewen, James W., 55
Longstreet, Wilma, 83
love, 5, 8, 17–18, 22, 27, 31, 39–40, 57, 62–63, 69, 74, 88, 92, 152, 154, 161, 163

Mann, Horace, 118–119
marketization/corporatization of education, 126n3, 152, 158
Marzano, Robert J., 121n3, 142n2
Maxwell, John C., 145
May, Rollo, 92
Mayeroff, Milton, 20–21
mentor, 61–62, 65, 69, 138, 142n1, 146–147, 155n1, 163
mind, 4, 14, 22, 25, 27, 31–33, 38, 41, 48, 54, 77, 83–85, 86n1, 98, 106, 117, 162–163
mindfulness, 14, 37
Moller, Gayle, 145–146, 149
monologue, 39, 97
Montessori, Maria, 104n2
Mother Teresa, 18–19
motivation, 14, 20, 38, 45, 61, 64, 86n2, 92, 104, 106, 133, 142n2, 162–163
multicultural education, 53, 55–57
multiculturalism, 57
multiple intelligence theory, 107

National Association for the Education of Young Children (NAEYC), 101, 129
Nation at Risk, 124, 126, 126n3
National Conference of Catholic Bishops, 154
National Council of Teachers of English (NCTE), 129, 137, 138
neurobiology, 31
neurons, 32–33, 34n1
neuroscience, 31
Niebuhr, Reinhold, 18
No Child Left Behind (NCLB), 124, 127n4, 131, 134, 135n3
Noddings, Nel, 20–21, 40
Nouwen, Henry, 19, 25, 152

ontology, 9
open-mindedness, 13, 16, 26, 54

opportunity, xiii, 57, 121n3, 154, 158–159

Palmer, Parker, ix, 4, 19, 40, 69–70
Parkay, Forrest W., xiii, 81, 87–88, 105–106
Perrone, Vito, 121, 121n5, 125, 126n1, 127n5, 132–133
patience, 20–21, 74
pedagogy, xiv–xv, 57, 68, 80n1, 97, 126, 154
persistence, 17, 21–22, 102–103
philosophy, 8–10, 83–85, 86n1, 98, 117, 119; of education, 5, 7–8, 10n1, 22, 27, 49, 85, 97
Piaget, Jean, 89–91, 99, 104n1, 107
Picasso, Pablo, 71
Pinar, William, 68, 165
plasticity, 33, 34n1
Plato, 83, 161
Pollock, Jackson, 71, 73
poverty, x, 15, 62, 124, 127n4, 150–152, 155n1
practitioner, 9, 26–27, 121n1, 147
preferential option for the poor, 154, 155n3
professionalization, 5, 147
psychology, 26, 31, 77, 83–88, 92–93, 93n1–93n2, 97, 101, 117–118, 145, 162–163
Pugach, Marleen C., 20–21, 44–46, 92
Purpel, David, 5, 18

Race to the Top, 124, 130–131, 134, 135n3
Ravitch, Diane, 129, 135n4, 151–152
reflection, ix, 8–9, 22, 25–27
reflective practice, 27–28
respect, 17, 19, 36, 38, 43–46, 46n1, 49, 51n1, 56–57, 64, 69, 78, 100, 146, 149
responsibility, 5, 5n1, 13, 16, 22, 26, 44, 49, 107, 138, 141, 147, 154, 158–159
Roberts, Peter, 9, 40
Robinson, Ken, 69
Rodham Clinton, Hillary, 159
Rogers, Carl, 92
Rohr, Richard, 105
Rose, Mike, 131

Rousseau, Jean-Jacques, 81, 83–86, 86n2, 104n2

Sacks, Peter M., 119–120, 121n3, 121n4, 126, 129, 131, 133
Sahlberg, Pasi, 149
Schön, Donald A., 26
Siegel, Daniel J., 31–38, 47–48
Sizer, Nancy F., 51n1
Sizer, Theodore R., 51n1, 129
Shor, Ira, 40
Skinner, B.F., 88–89
Slattery, Patrick, ix, 8, 68, 123–126, 165
Slavin, Robert E., 77, 79, 81, 88–89, 98, 101, 105–107
Socrates, x, 39, 118
Socratic method, 118
spirituality, 18, 162
Sputnik, 124
Stanford-Binet, 120
Steinberg, Shirley, ix, 8
stimulus-response, 87, 105
student-centered, 69–70, 99
Sullivan, Anne, 62–63, 65–67

teacher-centered, 98–99, 106
temperament, 13, 43, 157
tests, 114–121, 121n5–121n6, 123–125, 126n1–127n6, 129–134, 135n3, 137; high stakes, 115, 119–120, 124–125, 130–132, 141, 167; standardized, 114, 118–121, 123–126, 126n1, 127n5–127n6, 129–135; test anxiety, 132. *See also* assessment

theory, ix, 77–79, 80n2, 83, 87–92, 93n2, 100, 105–108, 119, 146, 165
Thorndike Handwriting Scale, 120
Thorndike, Edward L., 88, 117–118, 120, 121n1, 125, 127n5
tolerance, 15, 20, 65, 74
Tomlinson, Carol Ann, 100, 104n3
trust, 4, 18, 21, 40–41, 43–45, 47, 49–50, 51n1, 61, 91, 102, 149
Tyler, Ralph, 123, 126n2, 165

unfinishedness, 9–10, 26

village, 154, 155n1, 158–159
Vygotsky, Lev, 89, 91, 104n1, 107, 109n1

Watson, John B., 88
whole-heartedness, 13, 16, 54
Whitaker, Todd, 97
Wiggins, Grant, 113–114, 133, 137–138

About the Author

James D. Kirylo is professor of education at Southeastern Louisiana University. His published works include *Paulo Freire: The Man from Recife* and *A Critical Pedagogy of Resistance,* among other books and articles in a variety of professional journals.

www.ingramcontent.com/pod-product-compliance
Lightning Source LLC
Chambersburg PA
CBHW020737230426
43665CB00009B/474